Second Language Learners

STEPHEN CARY

Stenhouse Publishers

The Galef Institute

Strategies for Teaching and Learning Professional Library

Administrators: Supporting School Change by Robert Wortman
Assessment: Continuous Learning by Lois Bridges
Creating Your Classroom Community by Lois Bridges
Dance as a Way of Knowing by Jennifer Donohue Zakkai
Drama as a Way of Knowing by Paul G. Heller
Literature as a Way of Knowing by Kathy G. Short
Math as a Way of Knowing by Susan Ohanian
Music as a Way of Knowing by Nick Page
Second Language Learners by Stephen Cary
Writing as a Way of Knowing by Lois Bridges

Look for announcements of future titles in this series on science and visual arts.

Stenhouse Publishers
The Galef Institute

Library of Congress Cataloging-in-Publication Data
Cary, Stephen.
   Second language learners / Stephen Cary.
     p. cm.
   Includes bibliographical references.
   ISBN 1-57110-065-2 (alk. paper)
   1. Language and languages—Study and teaching. 2. Second language
   acquisition. I. Title
   P51.C339 1997
   418'.007—DC21
                                       97-29709
                                         CIP

Manufactured in the United States of America on acid-free paper.
13 12 11 10 09   14 13 12 11 10

Dear Colleague:

The extraordinary resource books in this series support our common goal as educators to apply best practices to everyday teaching. These books will encourage you to examine new resources and to discover and try out new and different teaching strategies. We hope you'll want to discuss and reflect on your strategies with other teachers and coaches in your support study group meetings (both face-to face and virtual) to make the most of the rich learning and teaching opportunities each discipline offers.

If we truly believe that all children can be successful in school, then we, must find ways to help all children develop to their full potential. This requires understanding of how children learn, thoughtful preparation of curriculum, reflection, adaptation of everyday practices, and ongoing professional support. To that end, the *Strategies for Teaching and Learning Professional Library* was developed. The series offers you countless opportunities for professional growth. Its rather like having your own workshops, coaching, and study groups between the covers of a book.

Each book in this series invites you to explore
  • the theory regarding human learning and development—so you know why,
  • the best instructional practices—so you know how, and
  • continuous assessment of your students' learning as well as your own teaching and understanding—so you and your students know that you know.

The books offer *Dialogues* to reflect upon your practices, on your own and in study groups. The Dialogues invite responses to self-evaluative questions, experimentation with new instructional strategies in classrooms, and perhaps a rethinking of learning philosophy and classroom practices stimulated by new knowledge and understanding.

Shoptalks with short, lively reviews of the best latest professional literature as well as professional journals and associations.

Teacher-To-Teacher Field Notes full of tips and experiences from other practicing educators who offer different ways of thinking about teaching practices and a wide range of successful, practical classroom strategies and techniques to draw upon.

It's our hope that as you explore and reflect on your teaching practice, you'll continue to expand your teaching repertoire and share your success with your colleagues.

Sincerely,

Linda Adelman Johannesen

Linda Adelman Johannesen
President
The Galef Institute

The Strategies for Teaching and Learning Professional Library is part of the Galef Institute's school reform initiative *Different Ways of Knowing.*

Different Ways of Knowing is a philosophy of education based on research in child development, cognitive theory, and multiple intelligences. It offers teachers, administrators, artists and other specialists, and other school and district educators continuing professional growth opportunities integrated with teaching and learning materials. The materials are supportive of culturally and linguistically diverse school populations and help all teachers and children to be successful. Teaching strategies focus on interdisciplinary, thematic instruction integrating history and social studies with the performing and visual arts, literature, writing, math, and science. Developed with the leadership of Senior Author Linda Adelman Johannesen, *Different Ways of Knowing* has been field tested in hundreds of classrooms across the country.

For more information, contact

The Galef Institute
11050 Santa Monica Boulevard, Third Floor, Los Angeles, California 90025
Tel 310.479.8883
Fax 310.473.9720
www.dwoknet.galef.org

Strategies for Teaching and Learning Professional Library

Contributors

President
Linda Adelman Johannesen

Senior Vice President
Sue Beauregard

Editors
Resa Gabe Nikol
Susan Zinner

Editorial Assistant
Elizabeth Finison

Editorial Consultant
Lois Bridges

Designer
Delfina Marquez-Noé

Photographers
Ted Beauregard
Dana Ross

A tip of the hat to all for the invaluable, Teacher-To-Teacher Field Notes.

Joyce Caudill
Laurel Cress
Amika Kemmler Ernst
David Freeman
Yvonne Freeman

Lisa Fulks
Etty Korengold
Roberta Lee
Leslie Mangiola
Wendy Motoike

Stefani Rosenberg
Lillian Utsumi
Carol Wright

A big thanks to David and Yvonne Freeman, Lillian Utsumi, and Carol Wright, for making time in their busy schedules to review the manuscript.

Finally, a special thanks to Lois Bridges and ARBM for support and encouragement throughout the project.   —SC

Special thanks to Andrew G. Galef and Bronya Pereira Galef for their continuing commitment to our nation's children and educators.

Contents

Chapter 1

Second Language Instruction

Teachers are a wonderfully diverse bunch of folks. We differ on everything from background and curriculum interests, to grade preference, management techniques, and teaching style. Regardless of the differences, however, we share a common, overarching goal: we all want to do right by kids. Teachers everywhere search for ways to include and invite all students into the world of learning. For kids who speak little or no English, we can now apply new understandings about how to open the door to their learning.

The last few years have brought major changes in second language learner (SLL) programs and practices. Change was spurred on, in part, by the dramatic increase in the numbers of second language learners across the country. With so many kids entering the system who speak little or no English, teachers, administrators, and state and local boards took a serious look at existing SLL services, and often found them wanting.

In the five-year span from 1987 to 1991, for example, California public schools saw a sixty-one percent jump in SLL growth. As I write this, nearly a quarter of all students in the California public schools are learning English as a second language (California Department of Education, *Language Census Reports* 1991, 1996). Demographic forecasters tell us the population of these students will continue to rise sharply in the coming years. For most teachers, the message in the numbers is simple: If you're working with some children who are second language learners right now, you'll be working with even more in the future. If you're not working with any such children right now, chances are good you will be soon.

As bedrock for rebuilding programs and practices, educators have turned to a large body of research interweaving the latest findings from several disciplines, including second language acquisition, bilingual education, cognitive psychology, brain physiology, and critical pedagogy. Shaped by this research, English as a Second Language (ESL) and English Language Development (ELD) programs are now more likely to be content- and literature-based rather than skills-driven. Communication-based learning events have replaced grammar-based activities. Primary language and Specially Designed Academic Instruction in English (SDAIE) are making learning events understandable for the first time to many of our second language learners. Getting a good hold on content is now as important a goal as getting a good hold on language. More and more teachers are achieving results with a student-centered, integrated-curriculum approach. Happily, this all means that more doors are opening, rather than closing, for our students.

According to the U.S. Census Bureau, as of April 1993, one in fourteen U.S. residents over the age of five speaks a language other than English at home, a thirty-five percent increase since 1980.

Even with all the positive changes, students with little or no English skills pose significant challenges for teachers—especially those new to teaching or new to working with these youngsters. Even teachers with Second Language Acquisition (SLA) training want to increase their stockpile of practical ideas that help students build both language and content.

This book offers teachers and administrators help in bringing all learners, at all levels of English language proficiency, into the core curriculum. It outlines a number of program models, offers some theory on how language is acquired, and provides a host of strategies and techniques for supporting all students in the classroom.

Though the book's examples target grades K-6, the strategies and techniques highlighted are just as applicable to middle and high school grades. Those same strategies and techniques can also be used with native English speakers in bilingual and foreign language programs. Helping both nonnative and native English speakers acquire a second language is consistent with the vision of *The National Standards in Foreign Language Education Project*, which is to have "all students develop and maintain proficiency in English and at least one other language, modern or classical."

As you implement some of the ideas here, you'll naturally encounter some stumbling blocks. Though the book provides advice on how to avoid problem spots, the best place to turn for more help is those talented folks around you—your colleagues. Peer-coaching partners can give personalized, long-term support, which is what most of us need in our continuing efforts to open the classroom door for our growing population of second language learners.

I try to practice what I preach—interaction. So, there's lots of room for you to jump in along the way, reflect, wrestle with the material, and put in your very important two cents. If you can, use the book with a colleague, grade-level team, or the entire faculty. Collaboration will offer you more solutions to common problems. Talk about what's here and also what's not. Add to the techniques, take an activity in a new direction. Make the book your own as you roll out the welcome mat for students.

The Name Game

In certain circumstances, labels can be helpful. They allow us to target a particular student or group of students. They can serve as reminders of where students are at a given point and help us plan appropriate instruction. For example, if I know a quarter of my class is at a low-proficiency stage, producing only short responses in English, then I know those students will benefit from a "jump-start" video clip for a literature book. But labels often do more harm than good. Unfortunately, some of the labels we've used for children who come into the system with little or no English skills have carried a negative message. Limited-English Speaking /Non-English Speaking (LES/NES) or Limited-English Proficient /Non-English Proficient (LEP/NEP) seem to emphasize what kids don't have—English fluency and proficiency. It's useful, instead, to emphasize what they're developing and what they *do* have—primary language skills and second language skills.

DIALOGUE

Are you slogging away each day in the "trenches" or nurturing grapes in the "vineyard?" Do you report to the "front line" for action or join your "family of learners" in the classroom? What metaphors are you hearing yourself and colleagues use to describe school? to describe students?

_____

_____

_____

How might a change in workplace labels (made by one person or even several people on a staff) make a difference in the lives of teachers and kids?

_____

_____

_____

So what do we call these students? My preference is students—just plain students. But as an option, let's go with second language learners, a positive term that emphasizes the students' growing resource advantage—having two languages instead of only one.

SHOPTALK

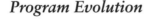

Gibbons, Pauline. *Learning to Learn in a Second Language.* Portsmouth, New Hampshire: Heinemann, 1993.

Learning to learn in a second language isn't impossible nor even difficult, provided that the classroom learning environment offers the support that enables language learning. Read this slim book and discover additional strategies and practical suggestions to help you create a responsive program that helps children learn a second language as they use that language to learn.

Program Evolution

Our programs for second language learners have gone through a number of significant changes over the last twenty-five years. Let's take a quick tour.

In the '70s, most second language learners moved mechanically through a separate ESL curriculum. A grammar-based, drill-heavy text, workbook, or prepackaged kit often provided the basis for interaction. What happened in a lesson depended for the most part on what a given scope and sequence said should happen. If this were the second week in September, it was almost sure to be Present Tense and Body Parts—*only* Present Tense and Body Parts. Many teachers were using objects and visuals to support lessons, but most kept to the "repeat-after-me" format.

Teachers emphasized the mastery learning of language and maintained, or struggled to maintain, large student and class profile cards. They crossed off dozens of little boxes on the cards as students were introduced to, and finally mastered, a mile-long list of discrete skills—everything from food vocabulary and the discrimination of phonemes, to consonant digraphs, possessive pronouns, and irregular plurals. Students needed to complete Box One, Skill One with a high degree of accuracy before moving on to Box One, Skill Two. Teachers stressed language form over message. Since a linear view of language development was the mode of thinking, listening and speaking skills needed to be in place before students could progress to reading and writing.

The upshot? A record-keeping nightmare for teachers, and mostly a snoozer and loser for students. Primarily, content was the English language itself. And very few eight year olds are genuinely enthusiastic about direct instruction on the correct placement of adjectives or a ten-minute substitution drill on the present progressive. Although second language learners certainly made progress in English in the '70s (perhaps in spite of instruction), gains were often meager.

Topics and themes began driving instruction in the 1980s. Content became meatier. Teachers de-emphasized language form and started concentrating more on language message. The goal was to have students gain fluency by using language for real communication. Instruction became more understandable for second language learners through Natural Approach (Krashen and Terrell 1983) and Sheltered Instruction methodology (Schifini 1988), two meaning-centered, communicative-based approaches for second language and content acquisition.

Out went elaborate grammar explanations, over-correction, flash cards, and drills. In its place was a low-anxiety environment with error acceptance and heavy use of real objects, models, and visuals. In addition, teachers grounded in the research of language acquisition were seeing language development in a new light. Listening, speaking, reading, and writing skills were interconnected and developed simultaneously. Beginning-level second language learners were often exposed to appropriate reading and writing activities. Becoming a proficient reader and writer of English was just as important as becoming a fluent speaker of English. Unlike the second language learning programs in the '70s, the SLL instruction of the '80s made an attempt to embrace *literacy*.

With instruction more comprehensible and engaging, kids started acquiring more language and more content. But though we'd replaced textbooks, grammar workbooks, and commercial kits with a thematic, literature-based approach, our second language themes and literature books never fully matched the curriculum of native English-speaking students. As in the '70s, second language learners were all too often in a world of curriculum separate from native English-speaking students, shuttling back and forth between two very different worlds of curriculum, one ESL, the other the mainstream classroom.

Topics and themes are still driving instruction, but now they're much more likely to match those of the mainstream curriculum.

Field Notes: Teacher-To-Teacher

This year, I refused to do the formal ESL program with my kinders that entailed flashing picture cards at them and recording the ones they could name in English. Instead, I've simply involved them in our classroom activities. As a result, all children showed significant language development progress, reflected in their Language Assessment standardized test scores. Some gained as many as thirty points on the test. They weren't getting ESL drills, so where did their newly-acquired English come from? From everyday, learner-centered classroom activities—shared reading with the whole class, dramatizing and discussing books in English, singing many, many songs in English, and participating in collaborative learning activities where they were seated with monolingual English speakers. And of course, they made friends with English-speaking children, played together in the playhouse, built block towers, and interacted with their English-speaking friends in any of a hundred ways in the classroom and on the playground.

Laurel Cress
Longfellow School
Hayward, California

In the '90s, we're striving to maintain and build on our earlier successes of the '80s. We're stressing communicative and academic competence over language mastery more than ever before, and using Natural Approach and SDAIE techniques throughout the grades and with students at all levels of English proficiency. Topics and themes are still driving instruction, but now they're much more likely to match those of the mainstream curriculum.

And because of our emphasis on meaning- and student-centered learning activities, topics and themes of today are more likely to hold high interest for students. Whenever we can, we're trying our best to integrate second language learners and students whose first language is English. We see fewer traditional ESL "pull-out" programs these days and more "push-in" programs that include resource people helping in the classroom.

DIALOGUE

Where would I place my own second language program (or my school's) in terms of era? (Some teachers and schools may share program elements from more than one era.) What are the elements that describe my program?

_____

_____

_____

What elements do I want to keep and expand? to eliminate? Are there any key "gotta have" elements missing from the list?

_____

_____

_____

We're responding to students' multiple intelligences, and, in turn, the literacy spectrum is expanding to help integrate second language learners into mainstream classrooms. Drawing on the work of Howard Gardner (1983, 1993), we're offering students different ways of learning—through music, dance, drama, and the visual and media arts. We're also inviting them to use the visual, media, and performing arts to show us what they have learned. As we expand the literacy spectrum in this way, we're no longer wholly dependent on written reports and essays for assessment. Instead, our

Field Notes: Teacher-To-Teacher

One of my most exciting recent discoveries is the value of tapping into childrens' multiple intelligences to help me—and them—assess their comprehension of literature. Students can choose to work alone, with a partner, or in a group. (They may also choose to work on their projects with a partner at home.) Students create a project that uses one or more of the seven intelligences and shows what they've learned about a story. For example, they may write a poem or a letter to a character (linguistic), make a chart or graph showing events in the story and the excitement level of each event (mathematical-logical), create and perform a dance or a play (bodily-kinesthetic), make a poster, diorama, puppets, or a game (spatial), or create a song or a rap (musical). Developing and sharing their projects formally with the class offers students wonderful means for oral language development. Natural opportunities abound for students to describe their process and their own creativity—orally, kinesthetically, and in written form. During project time, our classroom is alive with engaged students working, discussing, and enjoying their own and others' projects.

Wendy Motoike
Encinita School
Rosemead, California

students may explore mathematical concepts such as patterns and factorials through hands-on experiences with pennies, nickels, and quarters. (How many different ways can the coins be ordered?) They extend and refine their understanding of factorials when we read aloud *Anno's Mysterious Multiplying Jar* by Masaichiro and Mitsumasa Anno, show them slides of famous artwork that reflects mathematical patterns, and invite them to demonstrate their understanding of patterns and factorials through their own drawing, painting, or sculpture. We may even invite them to create a movement piece based on Anno's book. (How would you represent a factorial through movement?) Our evolving understanding of multiple intelligences and different ways of knowing is helping second language learners, and all our students, access the core curriculum.

Second Language Program Evolution at a Glance

Decade	Program Characteristics
1970s	• grammar-based curriculum • instruction based on text kits • language form stressed over message • "repeat-after-me" drills and continuous correction • skills checklists
1980s	• meatier curriculum, but not connected to mainstream curriculum • instruction based on topics and themes • language used for communication • Natural (developmental, low-stress) Approach and Sheltered (contextualized) Instruction • visuals and real objects aided instruction
1990s	• core curriculum topics and themes • meaning- and student-centered learning activities • multicultural perspective across the curriculum • theme-based reading and writing • language used for communication • Natural Approach and SDAIE techniques • access to multiple intelligences (expands the literacy spectrum) • free, voluntary reading time • primary language support and development • more integration of second language students with students whose first language is English • authentic assessment

There's also more emphasis today on voluntary reading for pleasure, critical thinking activities, and authentic assessment. And there is a growing recognition of the importance of supporting students' primary language development.

The Need for Long-term Primary Language Development

For years, studies on bilingual education have shown the critical connection between primary language skills and academic success. Second language students with a solid primary language foundation established in bilingual programs, consistently outperform second language students in non-bilingual programs—in both their primary language and in English. Indeed, research by Charles Leyba, Dorothy Legarreta, Jim Cummins, Muriel Saville-Troike, Laurene Burnham, Marilyn Peña, and Charles Herbert and others supports this need for long-term primary language development. Now, we also know that students who develop literacy and background knowledge in their first language learn English and subject matter taught in English more easily.

So how do we develop that primary language foundation? There are lots of possibilities, but which model is most effective? Unfortunately, the model that districts or schools choose often hinges on factors other than the

Second language students with a solid primary language foundation established in bilingual programs, consistently outperform second language students in non-bilingual programs—in both their primary language and in English.

evidence from research about what is best for kids. Short-term, transitional models are generally easier to sell to a community than long-term bilingual programs. Transitional, early-exit programs offer bilingual instruction only through grade two or three. With the Newcomer Center approach, children who recently arrived in the U.S. are placed in self-contained classrooms for intensive English language development and acculturation activities. Although these programs have enjoyed widespread popularity, large, longitudinal studies (Ramirez 1991; Collier 1992; Thomas and Collier 1995) provide strong evidence that the models with the most emphasis on primary language development are the ones where second language kids achieve the most—academically and in their second language. Specifically, Late-Exit Maintenance and Dual Immersion are the models that fit this bill. Let's take a look at them.

Bilingual Late Exit (Late Transition/Maintenance). The teacher or aide uses English and the students' primary language for instruction throughout the elementary grades. Though the percentage of first to second language instruction varies, this model provides long-term support and development in students' primary language, leading to literacy and academic competence in both first and second languages. Instructional delivery formats vary, depending on grade level and student needs. Using Spanish as the primary language, for example, formats might include

- alternate week instruction (one week English, the next Spanish)
- alternate day instruction (Monday English, Tuesday Spanish)
- modified alternate day (Monday mostly in English, Tuesday mostly in Spanish; general business, directions, and most activities in the target language of the day with some work—such as book groups, for example—in the other language)
- half-day, half-day (morning English, afternoon Spanish)
- alternate day subjects (Monday language arts in English, Tuesday in Spanish)
- preview-review (preview in Spanish, lesson in English, review in Spanish).

After fifth or sixth grade, students are usually placed in an all-English program. Maintenance programs sometimes continue bilingual instruction into middle and high school.

Dual Immersion (Two-Way Bilingual). This program is implemented in kindergarten or preschool. Students learning to speak English are integrated, often in a 50/50 split, with students who are monolingual English speakers.

All children gain a second language, but students learning English are introduced gradually to the language. In kindergarten, there is often a 90/10 split—ninety percent Spanish instruction, for example, to ten percent English instruction. Usually by sixth grade, instruction is fifty percent in the first language, and fifty percent in the second language. The goal is bilingualism and biliteracy for all students. Dual immersion schools, such as Fiesta Gardens in San Mateo-Foster City School District (northern California), are so successful and popular that parents often camp out at the school the night before registration to make sure their children enroll.

S H O P T A L K

Lessow-Hurley, Judith. *The Foundations of Dual Language Instruction*. New York: Longman, 1990.

If you're new to bilingual education and need a solid overview of the field, this is the book for you. In plain English that's free of educational jargon, Lessow-Hurley spells out the basics of dual language models, theory, and research. She also takes the reader on a fascinating armchair field trip, showing how the historical, cultural, legal, and political context has shaped and reshaped dual language instruction.

Instructional Models

Programs run the gamut on how much support they provide SLL students—from sink or swim all-English programs with no support to those with a strong primary language maintenance component. Let's take the tour.

Submersion ("Sink or Swim"). Students usually sink. Second language students are placed in an all-English classroom with all instruction geared to native English-speaking students. There is no primary language support, no English Language Development/English as a Second Language (ELD/ESL) support, and no contextualizing (sheltering) of instruction.

Standard ELD/ESL, Pull-out/Push-in. With pull-out programs, students are removed from the self-contained classroom to work with the ELD/ESL resource teacher or aide. Grouping is often homogeneous, meaning that all students are second language learners, and may all be at the same language acquisition stage. (See page 54 for information on Language Acquisition Stages.) With push-in programs, students work with support staff who come into the classroom. Push-in groups usually contain all second language learners but sometimes include one or two students who speak only English. Work is often done in a designated ELD/ESL corner of the room. With both types, frequency of instruction varies—from twenty to forty-five minutes per day to twenty to forty-five minutes two or three times a week. There is no communication or instruction in students' primary language. Instead, the focus is on oral English skills, "survival" English, beginning literacy, and school and community acculturation activities. The teacher often follows a commercial or district ELD/ESL scope and sequence curriculum. With pull-out and push-in, students typically operate in two disconnected worlds of learning—ESL and core curriculum—with one world only rarely supporting and nurturing the other.

Content-Based ELD/ESL, Pull-out/Push-in. Though this model emphasizes the development of basic English language skills like Standard ELD/ESL does, it also focuses on previewing, reviewing, and building the vocabulary, concepts, skills, and activities of the core curriculum. In both pull-out and push-in varieties, the resource person and classroom teacher plan together on a regular basis to ensure a cohesive, comprehensible, and inclusionary program for second language kids.

Content-Based ELD/ESL, Teacher-provided. More often than not, given the lack of human resources in so many schools, the regular classroom teacher is providing all the ELD/ESL instruction. Some teachers do daily ELD activities at a designated time just with their second language students. Others integrate ELD opportunities throughout the school day preferring to have their second language students develop second language skills as they work with native English speaking peers. And finally, some teachers combine a designated ELD time-slot with the integrated ELD route.

Regardless of the particular format, ELD/ESL is associated with second language learners having lower English language proficiency (acquisition stages 1, 2, and 3).

Newcomer Center. Recently arrived second language students are placed in a self-contained classroom for intensive English language development and acculturation activities. This program sometimes includes primary language support and development as well as a parent education component. The length of time students spend in a Newcomer Center varies. A cap is often set at six months to a year. Students exit into bilingual, SDAIE, or mainstream classes depending on availability.

SDAIE (Specially Designed Academic Instruction in English). SDAIE instruction helps second language students learn core curriculum content and expand English skills. The instruction is characterized by heavy use of manipulatives, visuals, videos, key vocabulary, collaborative learning, end-product modeling, role plays, and mindmapping. SDAIE, previously called Sheltered Instruction (Krashen 1985), was originally designed for homogeneously grouped secondary students at the intermediate fluency stage (stage 4). Large numbers of middle and high schools still follow the original format. What you see in many elementary classrooms today, however, is the application of SDAIE techniques (like storyboarding, role-plays, or a lesson preview via video, for example) with students at all proficiency stages. In fact, SDAIE techniques, sometimes called scaffolding techniques, are being used increasingly with native English-speaking students as well, since they help make instruction more concrete and understandable for all students.

The Big Three. Today's SLL programs come in all shapes and sizes. Most K-6 programs, however, offer students English Language Development (ELD) and instruction utilizing a variety of SDAIE techniques. Middle and high school programs provide ELD and designated SDAIE classes, for example, SDAIE

Although today's second language programs come in a variety of shapes and sizes, increasingly, the ideal second language program is offering "The Big Three"—ELD, SDAIE, and long-term, primary language support and development.

"The Big Three"

English Language Development

Who	Students at beginning and beginning-intermediate levels of language acquisition
What	Build fluency (Basic Interpersonal Communication Skills—BICS) and content learning
How	Students learn through their multiple intelligences, literature, and content-based thematic activities. Manipulatives, videos, CD-ROMs, photos, drawings, Total Physical Response (TPR), songs, chants, dance, and role-plays are used to support instruction.

Specially Designed Academic Instruction in English (SDAIE)

Who	Students at intermediate levels of language acquisition, but SDAIE techniques are increasingly used with all stages
What	Build Cognitive Academic Language Proficiency (CALP) and grade-level content learning
How	Students learn through their multiple intelligences and content-based thematic activities. Collaborative learning, manipulatives, visuals, videos, CD-ROMs, chalk-talks, graphic organizers, text tours, music, drama, dance, and storyboarding are used to support instruction.

Primary Language Instruction

Who	Students at all levels of English language acquisition
What	Build academic language proficiency in their primary language
How	Students learn through instruction in their first language.

Algebra or SDAIE American History. Increasingly, the ideal SLL program is offering "The Big Three"—ELD, SDAIE technique-based activities or classes, and long-term, primary language support and development.

Key SLL Program Components. Here are some elements to consider when planning and implementing a second language learner program.

Strive for...

- one content-rich curriculum
- ongoing assessment in first and second language
- reflection of home culture in classroom and school activities
- mainstreaming or integration of second language learners
- manipulative-based, interactive instruction
- teacher expansion of the literacy spectrum
- contextualized English instruction
- value, support, and development of primary language
- primary language materials provided for teachers
- teachers trained in second language acquisition theory, ELD, and SDAIE techniques
- teaching by bilingual instructional aides in students' primary language
- parent outreach through classes, interpreters, school-to-home bilingual communications.

Avoid...

- a separate curriculum for second language learners
- skills-based assessment that's not integrated with curriculum and instruction
- exclusion of home culture in classroom and school activities
- segregation of second language learners for much of the day
- textbook-driven, transmission-mode instruction
- overdependence on reading and writing activities for teaching and learning
- "sink-or-swim" English instruction
- devaluation of primary language—never using it for instruction
- absence of primary language materials for teachers
- untrained teachers
- having bilingual aides run dittos and underutilizing their language skills
- absence of parent outreach.

A Framework for Planning and Implementation

Developing, implementing, and keeping an effective SLL program in fine tune is no easy matter. Choosing the most appropriate instructional delivery model, ensuring consistent first and second language development, involving parents and community in the school program, and maintaining a meaningful, content-rich curriculum can challenge the most experienced team of teachers and administrators.

The following four-part framework may help make a tough job a little easier. Though primarily intended for district-wide or site-level program planning, implementation, and reviewing, the framework can be used by an individual teacher as well.

Four simple questions drive the planning, implementation, and review process. All four are a lot easier to ask than to answer!

1. What do we have?
2. What do we need?
3. How do we get what we need?
4. How do we know we're getting what we need?

What do we have? Have a committee (existing or ad hoc) look at your current SLL program. The committee should consider

- use of human and financial resources
- equal access to the core classroom curriculum
- primary language support and development
- expansion of the literacy spectrum through the multiple intelligences
- type and effectiveness of instruction
- type and effectiveness of assessment
- staff development needs and existing training
- grouping strategies for second language learners
- use of materials and equipment (multimedia reference sets, primary language materials, realia)
- degree of consistency with research and state and district policies
- how students' self-esteem needs are being met
- degree of parent and community involvement.

Hints

- To assure a broad-based committee, include students, parents, teachers, and administrators.

- Give the committee real decision-making power.

- Provide adequate time and resources for the committee to do its work.

Don't "reinvent the wheel." If you've already done all this through a Program Quality Review or site-development plan, skip it and move on!

What do we need? After answering the first question, the committee examines the research recommendations for second language students. It draws up a proposed ideal SLL program and gains consensus for moving forward with it. The proposed program identifies the areas that need to be changed and spells out how the changes should occur. Often the information is presented in chart format, like the one below.

Change Area	Change Needed
Parent Involvement	More interpreters at parent-teacher conferences
	More bilingual school-to-home written communications
Materials	Mini-resource center with visuals, realia, and thematic unit material packaged for check-out
Teacher Support	Volunteer or paid aide to maintain and manage mini-resource center

Hints

- Shoot for the stars—the ideal SLL program. Then, with one foot planted firmly on the ground, modify your plan so it's attainable in the real world of your financial and human resources.

- Have the committee regularly run ideas and concerns past the whole staff and site council and ask for input. It's important to get broad support so that program changes work.

How do we get what we need? Specifying who needs to do what by when will keep you on track for creating your ideal program. A simple action plan matrix, like the one on page 24, can be used.

Hints

- Keep the plan simple and short—list only the crucial items.

- Don't overload teachers with a thousand additional tasks.

- If teachers take on extra tasks, provide them with time to complete the work.

Action	Who	By
Develop and maintain a current list of interpreters in a variety of target languages	Resource teacher or parent volunteer	Nov. 1
Obtain space for a resource center	Site council	Dec. 1
Identify realia, visuals, videos, music tapes, CDs, and other resources needed for the resource center and begin collection	Teachers, parent volunteer team, and student helpers	Mar. 1

If teachers take on extra tasks, provide them with time to complete the work.

How do we know we're getting what we need? Evaluate your program implementation and its effectiveness at regular intervals. How many program changes have you made? In judging effectiveness, use the standard measures—language proficiency test gains, primary and second language standardized test scores, grades, and items such as

- authentic assessment measures (portfolios, projects, and performance-based tests that expand the literacy spectrum and showcase the multiple intelligences)
- increase in primary language support and development
- attitude and self-esteem inventories
- teacher reports on student adjustment to school
- number of behavior referrals and student absences
- involvement of parents and community
- student participation in extracurricular activities
- increase in number of teachers trained in second language acquisition theory and practice
- increase in mainstream participation.

Remember that every program takes time, energy, and money, and is continually evolving to meet the ideal.

Chapter 2

Effective Instructional Practices: an Overview

While you read through the classroom examples that follow, you'll notice that many of the recommended practices for children learning a second language parallel our recommendations for all students. The practices are based on research-informed, effective instructional strategies. Though all kids benefit from them, children learning a second language *depend* on these practices. Without them, school can be a confusing and frustrating place. With these practices, school makes sense for second language learners, and they join their classmates in learning throughout the day.

What Effective Teachers Do

Here is a set of instructional practices that will make a world of difference for second language students.

Show students what you mean when you give directions. For example, during a study on ancient China, instead of asking students to "inspect, draw, and create a name for one of the artifacts on the table," hold up a Chinese bamboo cricket cage and give it a long, careful look, then do a quick sketch of the object on an overhead transparency, and label it "House for Insects."

Be sure to use body language, facial expressions, and pantomime to supplement the use of objects and visuals.

Be sure to use body language, facial expressions, and pantomime to supplement the use of objects and visuals.

Show children what they will be learning and doing. If they are going to make something, show them what the final product might look like. During a mapping unit, you could say, "Here's one of the invented country maps that a group did last year. Look how they color-coded different landforms."

Build instructional context for students. Use objects, models, and multimedia to do this. For example:

- use pattern blocks to help solve word problems
- show a video or CD-ROM clip on Middle Eastern city and country life to build a sense of place
- view a wedding ceremony to demonstrate the concepts of ritual and symbolism
- give a chalk talk with quick drawings on the board, chart paper, or overhead projector, to amplify key points for a direct instructional piece on nutrition
- bring in real pizza toppings (and real pizzas!) to showcase the difference between combinations and permutations
- play taped background music to accompany a read-aloud (listen to 1920s jazz while reading *Nicholas Cricket*)
- examine real crickets to illustrate insect anatomy
- role-play an Underground Railroad escape to illustrate the concept of freedom.

Use a preview-review format. You'll find that a short preview before a class activity or direct instructional piece, along with a review afterward, can really help students who might otherwise be lost. Concept explanations can be given in the first or second language by the teacher or a bilingual instructional aide.

Preview-review provides additional time for hands-on experience which is crucial when you have a limited supply of materials. The format also provides a safe environment for students to raise questions and make responses. Second language learners who never or only rarely share during whole-class discussions because of "error anxiety," often blossom verbally in the comfort of a small, informal group.

Modify your speech. You'll want to make small changes that increase students' understanding of your speech without distorting it or making it sound unnatural. Use

- slightly slower speech if you're a super fast talker
- fewer complex sentences
- specific names in place of pronouns
- fewer fused forms (yannowhatImean?).

For more information regarding modified speech, see "Making Speech Easy To Understand" on page 74.

Provide more wait-and-think time. All students need time to absorb and assimilate new information, but this is especially true for students working in their second language. For example, you might say, "Before anybody answers, let's take a minute to think. Write your opinion down and share it with your partner. Then you can share your ideas with everybody."

Use idioms freely, but explain them when necessary. Teachers used to go out of their way to shield second language learners from idioms—those expressions whose meaning is different from the usual meanings of the words that make up the expressions—fearing that idiom-heavy speech would make English even harder to comprehend. The problem with this approach is that as teachers, our speech, like everyone else's, is idiom-heavy. If we over-monitor as we talk, deleting idioms, we run the risk of speaking in a synthetic and unnatural way. Worst of all, we rob students of the chance to acquire idiomatic speech, the vehicle for so much of the color, charm, richness, and power of any language. The solution is to let idioms roll off the tongue—or off the printed page—and then offer an explanation of the idiom through a paraphrase whenever needed. After using the phrase "taken to the cleaners" and seeing several puzzled faces, you can offer a quick follow-up: "In other words, they cheated the man. His pockets were cleaned out—no money left!"

Imagine not providing students with idioms. In terms of language acquisition, we might really upset students' applecart, put them behind the eight ball, and keep them in the dark 'til the cows come home. They could find themselves up the creek without a paddle and paying through the nose because we didn't want to talk straight from the hip and give them language that was the real McCoy, language that could help them go the distance and bring home the bacon through thick and thin.

Field Notes: Teacher-To-Teacher

I once had a large collection of moms at my classroom door. I turned and told my kinders to "take your seats, I'll be right with you." I talked to the last mom, then I turned to my class. They were coming at me en masse with their chairs. I was at a loss as to what they were doing until one child asked, "Where should we take our seats?"

Carol Wright
William Anderson Elementary
Lawndale, California

Use lots of synonyms, paraphrasing and summarizing. For example, if you notice that some of your students look lost after you've used the word *dilemma,* help them by explaining, "That was a dilemma for the main character. Julie was in a very difficult situation. She didn't know what she should do."

Check often for comprehension. Ask yourself, "Am I really getting through?" There are several strategies that will enable you to check for comprehension in a nonintrusive way. Invite your students to

- give hand signals—thumbs up if they comprehend the material, thumbs down if they become lost
- use a journal to explain a concept—in their journals, students can discuss what they have learned, ask questions about the topic, or make connections to new ideas
- explain the directions to a partner or explain the activity of the moment
- use colored 3 x 5 cards—green side up means, "I understand, please continue" and the red side means, "Please stop to explain, I'm having trouble understanding."

Integrate students' interests, backgrounds, and home country experiences into activities. During an insect anatomy lesson, for instance, encourage a Vietnamese student to share stories he's heard from his grandparents about keeping crickets.

In Joyce Caudill and Lisa Fulks' classroom at Kenwood Elementary School in Louisville, Kentucky, students shared part of their ancestry during their study of immigration.

> We asked students to bring in their baby blankets, which some had received from an ancestor. Students wrote stories and drew pictures of their blankets, then shared their stories and blankets with the class. As part of our study, we invited three speakers—from El Salvador, Lebanon, and China—to our classroom to tell their immigrant stories.

Modeling your thinking and writing process will help students with their own writing.

Write in front of students. Modeling your thinking and writing process will help students with their own writing. Demonstrate writing a personal piece, using an overhead projector as you write, or sit at a computer with students watching a large monitor. Think out loud as you plan what to write. "I think I need to trade a couple of these weak words for stronger words so people will know how really heartbroken I was when my cat, Milly, died." When students see that even you revise your writing, they'll be less frustrated at their own first attempts.

SHOPTALK

Graves, Donald H. *Writing: Teachers and Children at Work*. Portsmouth, New Hampshire: Heinemann, 1983.

This may be the book that started it all—the one that revolutionized everything we know about writing and the teaching of writing. Graves explains the writing process and how to make it work in the classroom. He strongly recommends that teachers write, since it's much easier to work with student writers if we understand our own writing. Graves also insists that there is practically no limit to what kids can do as writers. "At every single point in our research," he writes, "we've underestimated what kids can do."

Offer students nontraditional assessment options. Imagine you and your class have been exploring and discussing some strategies for resolving conflict with "difficult" people. Instead of giving students a traditional pencil-and-paper test, invite them to create a peace-making project to show what they've learned. Students might role-play with a partner, script and audiotape a play, or summarize—verbally or in writing—a newspaper article dealing with conflict resolution in the local community.

Keep expectations high but reasonable. Teachers with high expectations for students communicate with words and actions that students can and will learn. However, you'll want to temper your high expectations with an understanding of your students' linguistic and academic development. Fourth grader Maricela is new to the United States this year and had just two years of schooling in Mexico. Of course she isn't expected to read an English literature book on her own, synthesize it, and make literature log entries in English that explain the author's craft in building sympathetic characters. So what do we expect of Maricela? First, we make sure that she has a bilingual buddy as a helper and a Spanish edition of the book we're reading (if available), or verbal or written summaries of chapters in Spanish. Then we expect her to take an active role in her book group, participate in discussions, keep literature logs in Spanish, and sketch-draw some thoughts with Spanish and eventually English labeling.

What Successful Students Do

While students are acquiring their second language, they can be full participants in the life of the classroom.

They participate in the class curriculum in a variety of ways. Nguyet, a second language learner in third grade, is at the front of the class with other students from her literature book group, acting out a key scene from Beverly Cleary's *Ramona and Her Father*. Nguyet is in a soak-up-the-language, pre-production (pre-speech) stage in English. Though she plays one of the main characters in the scene, she does not need to speak English. She is a "quiet teller"—a shadow actor speaks the necessary lines, while Nguyet uses pantomime and props, responding to the commands and directions that the story narrator and fellow actors give her.

They work in both heterogeneous and homogeneous groups. Heterogeneous groups contain monolingual English speakers along with second language students. The second language learners may have different primary languages and be at different English language acquisition stages. Homogeneous groups, often comprised of second language students with the same primary language, may meet for instruction in their primary language, ELD activities, and preview-review mini-sessions.

They talk and interact. Students work in pairs and small cooperative groups. And yes, it will be a bit noisy a good part of the time with so much talking and interacting going on. We hope it's on-task noise, and chances are it will be if we've set in place high-interest, easy-to-understand activities. But (I hear you groaning) it won't all be on-task noise. Sometimes that noise is just plain visiting, pure and simple, which can be a bitter pill to swallow for some folks. Here's the sugar coating: Even off-task visiting with English-speaking models can help second language students acquire language. And visiting can help initiate and cement friendships across ethnic, cultural, and language lines. Indeed, as Lawndale, California, teacher Carol Wright says, "I often find that the 'noise' in my classroom is a lot more constructive than it may first appear."

Field Notes: Teacher-To-Teacher

My students really get into dissecting clams, observing worms, and hatching chicks. When we have hands-on science, second language learners are paired with their native English-speaking peers. Pairing naturally facilitates talking—and kids want to talk! The most exciting thing is that so much grows out of their talking—note-taking, writing, drawing pictures, asking questions, becoming acquainted with different languages, and truly engaging in their learning.

Amika Kemmler Ernst
Manning Elementary School
Boston, Massachusetts

They *have* language buddies, and they *are* language buddies. Language buddies are a wonderful way to bridge the language gap. Their benefit is two-fold. Language buddies help their peers understand you and help you better understand your second language learners. Consider the following scenarios. Blas, a bilingual second grader, sits at a table beside new student Eduardo. Eduardo missed most of the directions to the math puzzle center, so Blas, Eduardo's language buddy, speaks in Spanish and fills him in on what to do. In another situation, you're demonstrating capillary attraction using a twisted handkerchief connecting two containers positioned at different levels—the higher one holding colored water, the lower one empty. Shigeo makes a hypothesis in Japanese about what he thinks will happen to the water in the higher container if it is left in that position overnight. Then he signals his language buddy, Hiroko, and Hiroko translates.

Field Notes: Teacher-To-Teacher

I teach fifth grade in Fair Oaks Elementary School in Redwood City, California. As ninety percent of our student population is Latino, we offer a Spanish-English bilingual program that encourages most students to transition into English instruction by fourth grade. For several years now, we've been teaming fourth and fifth graders with kindergartners in very successful learning partnerships. Twice a week, the older children meet with their kinder buddies and participate in a number of literacy experiences with them. The older students read stories aloud to their young friends and encourage them to read back, they have written conversations about books or anything the five year olds want to chat about (through writing), and they act out stories with puppets or quick improvisations. Sometimes they use English, other times they rely exclusively on Spanish. The learning benefits for both older and younger students are evident: both experience the joy of using oral and written language to learn, and, in the process, grow in their abilities as flexible, adaptable language users—in two languages!

Leslie Mangiola
Fair Oaks School
Redwood City, California

Sharing their knowledge enables students to build on what they know, adding to their confidence as learners and teachers.

They serve as "home country experts." Sharing their knowledge enables students to build on what they know, adding to their confidence as learners and teachers. Let's say your class is studying architecture. Working collaboratively in groups, students collect information from each other. Chow sketches and labels his drawing of houses in Cambodia, while Arturo talks about his neighborhood in Honduras. When studying customs and holidays, a teacher asks her students to share their wealth of information. "Victor, in Mexico, what exactly happens on *Día de los Muertos*? What do people do? Jessica was wondering if it's a little bit like Halloween."

They expand their literacy spectrum. We invite our students to explore new concepts in a variety of ways. While examining the conflict leading up to the Revolutionary War, for example, we may read aloud to our students, invite them to look at visually rich texts such as *Colonial Living*, written and illustrated by Edwin Tunis, and then act out the conflict, create a dance piece demonstrating conflict through movement, or paint a dramatic mural that reflects the timeline of inflammatory events. They might also listen to music from that period and bring in songs from other wars. How do the battle songs of the Revolutionary War compare to those of the Civil War? World Wars I and II? How did the Vietnam War change things?

Field Notes: Teacher-To-Teacher

In my classroom, I have been using literature with young immigrant characters of the same age and cultural background of students in my class. My students are motivated because they can respond to the literature in personal and meaningful ways. In written reflections, students often express the enjoyment they feel when we read these books and they relate to the characters' immigrant experiences. They become our classroom experts on the country and culture of the characters in the story. I noticed that students showed pride in their own cultures and became more appreciative of the cultural diversity of our classroom.

Wendy Motoike
Encinita School
Rosemead, California

They move from the concrete to the abstract. When children study elements of physical geography, such as islands and mountains, they might first see a *National Geographic* video and then create islands and mountains through movement. How would you and your students show a mountain? Students might be encouraged to create such elements in sketches, with clay, or with papier-mâché. You might also have a science station set up for kids to experiment with water and floating objects. Students could then see additional video clips, read about different landforms in your state and in their home countries, and compare and contrast their discoveries.

They take "text tours" to increase their comprehension. Before students read a book section on air and water pollution, for example, guide them to extract as much information as they can from the text's photos, drawings, diagrams, charts, and boldface headings. Students use graphic organizers with visuals—also known as mindmaps, webs, and bubble maps—to take notes, summarize, outline, and brainstorm ideas. The visual organization of small bits of information helps students build a conceptual bridge to the written text.

As part of their effort to understand English material, second language students can read in alternative ways. They can

- read with a partner
- read along with an audiotape (commercial tapes or those created by you or your students)
- read a first language translation
- read via an oral or written, first or second language summary.

Noe Padilla in Wayne Lindse's fourth-fifth grade class at West Marin School in Pt. Reyes Station, California, created a drawing of the four key action points from the book *My Aunt Otilia's Spirits,* a humorous contemporary tale of the supernatural, that he used when the class discussed the book in small and large groups.

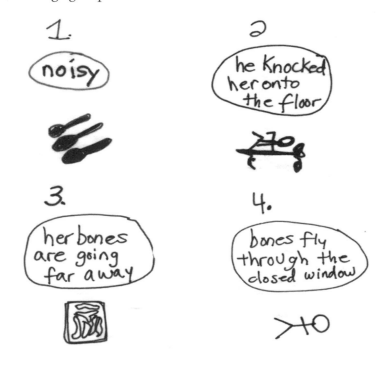

They make and use key vocabulary word banks. For example, if you're studying family customs, first and second graders can write down and illustrate words about eating activities. Students choose some words and then you'll add a few key words to the list. Some students like to organize their information using index cards that they file in a box. They may also use a designated section of a loose-leaf notebook for organization. Others add words to the butcher paper lists on the classroom walls. One class word bank might list all the breakfast items the students eat, another may focus on the typical breakfast foods in Vietnam. Remind and show students that most words in a word bank need an accompanying visual, like a drawing or magazine cut-out, to make it come alive.

manzana
apple

S H O P T A L K

Marks-Tarlow, Terry. *Creativity Inside Out: Learning through Multiple Intelligences.* New York: Innovative Learning Publications, Addison-Wesley, 1996.

ESL teacher Wendy Motoike says, "*Creativity Inside Out* is a practical, flexible resource guide that can be used to nurture multiple intelligences and creative expression. The book's layout is visually appealing, and its pages invite experimentation. Marks-Tarlow explains how to develop a creative classroom environment and build on the connections between creativity and self-esteem. Students are given opportunities to enhance skills, intelligences, and creativity through a variety of student groupings—cooperative learning, pair work, and whole class. Lessons have step-by-step instructions and creativity indexes offer an easy guide for developing units or for experimenting with the multiple intelligences in the classroom. The indexes are organized by subject, multiple intelligence, student configuration, time, special needs, and grade level. After a teacher has read this book and has begun to implement its concepts, the benefit for students is creativity-based learning that has unlimited possibilities. All students are regarded as talented in different ways and the focus is to enhance everyone's intelligence, even teachers'."

Later, students consult their individual and class word banks and make "withdrawals" when they write invitations and menus for the international foods luncheon they're hosting at the end of the month. For this and other theme-related activities, the word banks provide students with a "place to go for language."

A cautionary note on word banks: they can be overdone and misused. If we're not careful, they can easily turn into mile-long lists of unrelated words that students believe should be memorized. Students may also fall into the look-up-the-word and copy-the-definition trap, ending up with page after page of incomprehensible text. I remind students to "deposit" only those words that are personally meaningful—ones they understand and really want to use.

SHOPTALK

Wiesner, David. *Tuesday*. New York: Clarion Books, 1991.

Tafuri, Nancy. *Junglewalk*. New York: Greenwillow Books, 1988.

Collington, Peter. *The Angel and the Soldier Boy*. New York: Dragonfly Books, 1987.

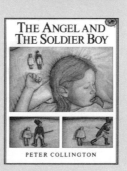

These are three of my favorite wordless picture books, filled with the sort of enticing artwork and subject matter guaranteed to get first and second language learners talking and writing up a storm. Inquisitive, flying frogs populate *Tuesday*. In *Junglewalk*, we tag alongside a young boy as he explores the world of toucans, crocodiles, parrots, and gorillas. Pirates rob a piggybank in *The Angel and the Soldier Boy*, and it's up to a courageous little angel doll to recover the loot and save a kidnapped toy soldier. With beginning second language learners, you may find it helpful to do one or two preliminary activities, such as a video or art project, that introduce some of the vocabulary in an upcoming wordless book. This will help students when they want to give the picture book an oral or written storyline. An alternative is to pair a beginning second language learner with a more English-proficient classmate and have them create and write the storyline together.

Word banks provide students with a "place to go for language."

In Wayne Lindse's fourth-fifth grade class at West Marin School in Pt. Reyes Station, California, students used their word banks to describe how to make cheese after doing it themselves first. Here's one student's description.

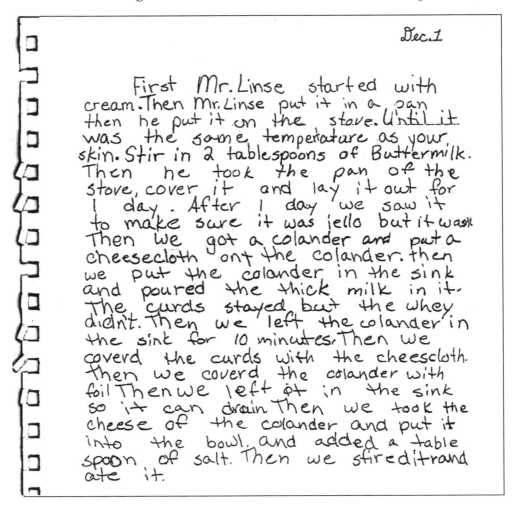

There are also alternative ways to write. Students can

- write in their first language
- transition write—doing some writing in their first language and some in their second
- progressive write—moving from drawings to labeling to writing text
- dictate to the teacher using a language experience approach—using talk that springs from high-interest, in- and out-of-class experiences to help students bridge from speaking to writing. The teacher typically "captures" and records the talk (or dictation) on chart paper during small and large group discussions.
- rely on a peer scribe—a second language learner dictates to a peer who speaks and writes English
- participate in partner writing—a second language learner writes with a peer who speaks and writes English.

A Tale of Two Classrooms

At first glance during my California Program Quality Review visit, the two classrooms appeared identical. Walk out of one, go across the hall into the other, and you'd swear you'd never left the first room. Both were third grade and had about the same gender and ethnic mix of students. Both had kids at tables working in small groups. Both rooms were exploring a topography theme (heavy on the volcanoes), so I saw a lot of the same activities and similar student work posted on the walls. The similarities extended to the teachers themselves—both were experienced, organized, energetic, and kid-loving. The only difference between the classrooms seemed to be how the doors were painted—one was yellow, the other blue. Subsequent observations, however, showed how substantially different the two classrooms really were.

One teacher integrated her second language and English-speaking students in most activities throughout the day even though some second language learners, she admitted, might initially understand a small percentage (say ten to twenty-five percent) of particular activities. She was willing to live with that low percentage because she had found the student integration led to more interaction, hence more opportunities to use language, more content learning, and most importantly, higher self-esteem for second language learners. Heterogeneous grouping was a must, she explained, because with it, second language students felt like full-fledged "citizens" of the classroom.

In stark contrast, the other teacher separated her second language students from their English-speaking peers for most of each day. At a special ESL table in a corner of the room, students moved through an ESL curriculum, working on survival-skill oral vocabulary, completing pages in a series of graded ESL workbooks, and sometimes listening to commercially taped stories, with periodic help from the teacher and aide.

This teacher reported that her second language students were consistently getting at least eighty to ninety percent of the ESL curriculum. English-speaking and second language students were together only for activities that the teacher felt second language students could understand without frustration, such as art and physical education. The teacher believed that the regular curriculum was way out of reach for kids with limited-English proficiency.

I was curious to know what her second language students thought about their "separate-but-equal" curriculum, and asked one of the boys in Spanish to tell me about the ESL work he was doing. He answered, "*Pues, piensa la maestra que no pueda hacer el trabajo regular—pero yo puedo.*" (The teacher thinks I can't do regular work—but I can.) I asked him what sort of work he'd like to do. Without hesitation, he answered with enthusiasm: "*¡Ciencia!*"

(Science!) I left him while he was filling in the blanks on a workbook page called, "How Many Do You Have?" (I have two eyes. I have one nose. I have two arms. I have ten fingers.) I've often wondered if that little guy ever got to do any science.

D I A L O G U E

What instructional practices would I like to use more often with my second language learners? Why?

_____

_____

What new practices interest me?

_____

_____

A Curriculum for Effective Second Language Learner Instruction

Four key elements characterize a curriculum for effective second language learner instruction.

1. Subject areas are integrated.
2. Information and concepts are accessible to children.
3. It is student-centered.
4. It is cognitively demanding.

Integration. The curriculum is integrated in the standard sense of connecting science to math to history to language arts, and also in connecting English language development to all learning events across the curriculum. The vocabulary and structures associated with beginning level, conversational English (Basic Interpersonal Communication Skills—BICS), as well as the literacy skills associated with higher level academic English (Cognitive Academic Language Proficiency—CALP), are developed through curriculum topics and material involving the entire class.

Accessibility. Students have supports—primary language instruction, language buddies, use of their multiple intelligences, manipulatives, visuals, task modeling, and chalk talks—that help them learn. They are exposed to the same topics and concepts in the curriculum as English-speaking students and are active members of the classroom's family of learners. They don't sit on the academic sidelines day after day with the curriculum flying two miles over their heads. Schoolwork makes sense; it is meaningful and doable.

S H O P T A L K

Freeman, Yvonne S. and David E. Freeman. *Whole Language for Second Language Learners*. Portsmouth, New Hampshire: Heinemann, 1992.

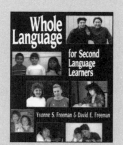

Full of language stories and examples of student work, this book is both enjoyable and essential reading for teachers of second language learners. It details how to create learner-centered classrooms that will support all learners—especially nonnative speakers of English. Readers will learn about ESL and bilingual methods, second language acquisition, and the importance of the first language and culture of all students. Teachers will find especially helpful the ideas for organizing the curriculum on a daily and long-term basis. The sample lesson plans are equally useful.

Student-centered. Students' culture, background, and interests are valued and incorporated into the curriculum. Learning events build on students' prior knowledge and skills. Moreover, all students act as resident tutors and resources.

Cognitively demanding. The curriculum challenges kids but does not overwhelm them. Students are exposed to grade-level curriculum whenever possible, but the curriculum starts where second language learners really

D I A L O G U E

How would I rate my own (or my school's) curriculum?

	Not At All	Partially	Fully
Integrated	☐	☐	☐
Accessible	☐	☐	☐
Student-centered	☐	☐	☐
Cognitively demanding	☐	☐	☐

What evidence supports my ratings?

_____

_____

_____

are (not where a scope and sequence committee would like them to be) and builds from there. Here's an example:

Susana is a fifth grader, new to the United States. Susana missed three years of schooling in El Salvador. She is interested in the physical science experiments on liquids, but is unfamiliar with the basics of measuring, a key background skill for an upcoming experiment. The teacher asks Elena to take Susana over to the sink for a "jumpstart" on liquid measure before tomorrow's science activity. Using a graduated beaker, Elena shows how to quantify and record different amounts of liquid, then lets Susana try some measuring herself. For Susana, working on a lower grade-level skill (measuring liquids) is critical. It's fun and interesting, and it helps lay the groundwork for success with more "officially designated" grade-level science work.

With a colleague, discuss program implementation problems and solutions. For example, if you'd like to build context by using more objects, models, and multimedia, explore how to get around the problems of manipulatives and equipment shortages, and of having too little time for finding materials.

DIALOGUE

How do I work with colleagues and parents to create an effective second language program for our school?

_____

_____

_____

What areas of my second language program need more attention?

_____

_____

_____

What one item, if attended to fully, holds the most promise for helping children who are learning a second language?

_____

_____

_____

What Effective Administrators Do

How principals support and guide their schools is critical to the success of the whole school community. Here is a list of administrative strategies that help teachers, students, and parents.

Collaborate with faculty. Share the decision-making power! The principal works collaboratively with teachers to develop policy and programs that help all students succeed. These joint efforts include designing, implementing, and monitoring a comprehensive staff development plan. The plan focuses on helping staff acquire the knowledge, strategies, and techniques needed for effective SLL instruction. Peer coaching is a fundamental part of the plan.

Participate in professional development. The whole staff, including the principal, needs to stay current on effective practices for second language learners.

Supervise and evaluate to help teachers reflect on their practices. The administrator supervises and evaluates teachers based on understanding what effective instruction for second language learners looks and sounds like in the classroom.

How principals support and guide their schools is critical to the success of the whole school community.

Offer ongoing support to teachers. Teachers are provided the materials they need to do the job, release time for planning and peer coaching, and if requested, videotaping of lessons. Mentor and resource teachers are available to demonstrate key strategies and techniques. Administrators also make sure teachers have the human resource support needed—language proficiency testers, bilingual instructional aides, parent and university primary language volunteers, and cross-age tutors.

Provide ample opportunities for home-school interaction. The school or district provides bilingual home-school communications such as board minutes, principal or teacher newsletters, and information on after-school activities to parents of second language learners. Interpreters are available for back-to-school night, child-study team meetings, parent-teacher conferences, site council meetings, and other important functions.

Ongoing and periodic day and night classes offer parents the chance to learn

- English and improve their primary language literacy skills
- what happens (and what doesn't) in the typical classroom
- how to support the school program at home
- what to do if their child has a problem at school
- how to access social services
- how to find local employment and employment training opportunities.

For more information on what successful administrators do, see *Administrators: Supporting School Change*, by Robert Wortman, in the Strategies for Teaching and Learning Professional Library.

SHOPTALK

Wortman, Bob. *Administrators: Supporting School Change*. Strategies for Teaching and Learning Professional Library, The Galef Institute. York, Maine: Stenhouse Publishers, 1995.

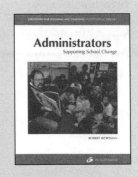

Bob Wortman gives a personal and convincing account, sharing his goals, vision, and strategies as an elementary school principal. Enthusiastically, Wortman explains how he strives to create a learning community that includes students, teachers, and administrators, as well as family members, support personnel, and the neighborhood beyond the school doors. You'll walk through a day in Wortman's life, seeing how a principal can have a positive impact on the lives he touches. This book is an easy and inspiring read, and one that you'll want to add to your personal shelf—whether you're a teacher or administrator.

Chapter 3

Connecting Theory and Practice

Second language theory and practice are interwoven in this chapter. After all, looking at theory without hooking it to practice is a lot like reading recipes but never getting to cook or taste a good meal. Without connecting theory and practice, teaching, like the food, stays abstract and untested. Practice helps us to visualize what good teaching and learning look like. But beware—practice without a base in theory is just plain hit-or-miss teaching, like trying to replicate some tasty, complex restaurant dish but getting only one or two ingredients right.

Finally, to torture the food analogy one last time, good cooks, like good teachers with lots of practice and understanding of the research, aren't afraid to jump in and go in a new direction, vary the recommended steps a little, or substitute one item for another here or there. Theory, especially second language acquisition theory, suggests a number of well-defined strategies for teaching second language learners. Effective and creative teachers, however, will take those strategies and interpret and reinterpret them in all sorts of different ways.

"The Magic 7" Elements of an Effective Program

A pattern emerges as you read through the many studies on second language acquisition. Successful programs share a number of the same guiding principles. My colleague, Connie Williams, and I took the essence of this research and developed a list of effective practices for teachers called "The Magic 7."

"The Magic 7" Guiding Principles

Optimal Condition	Implications for Teachers
1. Low-anxiety environment	Keep kids relaxed so that they are willing to take risks with language.
2. Comprehensible input	Make sure instruction is easy to understand for nonnative speakers.
3. Communication focus	Ask kids to use language for meaningful, real communication purposes.
4. Contextualized language	Provide context, backdrop, and concrete referents for language with objects, models, visuals, videos, maps.
5. Error acceptance	Model standard spoken and written English instead of overcorrecting through pronunciation drills and grammar exercises.
6. Respect for language stages	Make sure activities are developmentally appropriate.
7. Teacher is facilitator and co-learner	Be a "guide on the side" instead of a "sage on the stage." Encourage student inquiry and small group collaboration.

Magic 7 concept developed by Connie Williams and Stephen Cary, based on Krashen and Terrell (1983).

The premise is simple: the more of these principles we practice in the classroom, the bigger the gains in language and content for our second language learners.

If you look closely at the Magic 7, you'll see a striking parallel to the conditions that existed for all of us as we acquired our first language. Research strongly suggests that teachers can best help kids acquire their second language in the same sort of way that parents helped their children acquire their first (Krashen 1982, 1994).

The Natural Approach

The Magic 7 incorporates the key principles of Tracy Terrell's and Stephen Krashen's Natural Approach (Terrell 1977; Krashen and Terrell 1983) to second language instruction.

The Natural Approach emphasizes

- using language for meaningful communication
- message over form, and comprehension over production
- making messages (our teaching) easy to understand
- keeping kids as stress-free as possible
- paying attention to the developmental stages of language
- allowing students a silent period
- never forcing language production.

Take another look at the Magic 7's Implications for Teachers. When we allow new second language learners to answer by pointing or drawing, when we encourage a student to share an opinion by bridging through a bilingual class-mate, when we correct jumbled syntax through modeling, or use a video clip to help students better understand an upcoming lesson on world trade, we're teaching with the Natural Approach.

Over the years, Natural Approach teachers have significantly modified their view on literacy development. Though Krashen and Terrell (1983) stressed how important reading could be for second language students in generating easy-to-understand messages or comprehensible input, many teachers originally took the approach's oral communication focus to mean that reading and writing should be delayed until listening and speaking skills were in place. Today, Natural Approach teachers involve their second language students at all stages of English proficiency in meaningful and comprehensible literacy activities.

Krashen (1993) continues to emphasize the critical role of reading in second language development, and encourages teachers to give students large chunks of time for free voluntary reading in a relaxed setting. This type of reading requires a classroom library continually stocked with a wide variety of reading material.

DIALOGUE

Think about what you're doing at home to help your kids get a good hold on language. Or think of friends with children and how these parents are helping their young ones develop language. For each of the Magic 7 elements, list one specific "home front" first language example from your experience.

1. Low-anxiety environment

_____

2. Comprehensible input

_____

3. Communication focus

_____

4. Contextualized language

_____

5. Error acceptance

_____

6. Respect for language stages

_____

7. Teacher as facilitator and co-learner

_____

Would you be able to replicate all of these in the classroom with second language learners?

_____

_____

What modifications, if any, might you suggest as the examples are translated to the school setting?

_____

_____

_____

Students can use literature books, class story and poetry anthologies, magazines, newspapers, catalogs, advertisements, recipes, pamphlets, cereal boxes, comics, sports cards, and joke books. With a library like this, students at any proficiency stage can find material that's interesting and easy to understand. What's the specific payoff for kids with regard to free voluntary reading? According to Krashen, students build vocabulary and improve their spelling, grammar, and reading comprehension, sometimes more than during direct instruction if they're given time to read material of their own choosing. Not a bad deal!

Field Notes: Teacher-To-Teacher

As a resource teacher some years back, I observed a third-grade teacher in the middle of a science activity trying out a few phrases in Spanish that she'd picked up from her kids. The teacher's pronunciation was far from perfect and her verb endings needed some radical surgery. No matter—she valiantly pushed ahead and got the basic message out.

The kids responded with smiles and words of encouragement. One boy (without ever having attended one workshop on the importance of error acceptance and modeling) asked a question incorporating one of the phrases the teacher had really blown. The teacher answered, this time doing a little better with the phrase. In the same room a few days later, one Latina girl proudly handed me a story to read that she'd written in English. She told me in Spanish that it might be hard to read. Before I had the chance to say that I understood, she told me it was okay. She added that she would get better—just like her teacher would get better with Spanish.

– SC

Teachers calling themselves Natural Approach teachers these days use an eclectic mix of instructional strategies and techniques, practices not automatically or historically associated with teaching second language learners.

The Natural Approach is now a five-star umbrella term. Teachers calling themselves Natural Approach teachers these days use an eclectic mix of instructional strategies and techniques, practices not automatically or historically associated with teaching second language learners. The mix includes

- integrated, thematic instruction
- multisensory, multimedia teaching accessing students' multiple intelligences
- collaborative learning

- literature studies
- the language experience approach
- process writing; student publishing
- interactive journals
- manipulative-based math
- math discussions and journals
- hands-on, project-based science
- history/social science simulations.

Field Notes: Teacher-To-Teacher

As a bilingual teacher, I've started using parallel versions of literary works in Spanish and English. Recently, I used a popular Appalachian counting song for primary language instruction and ESL lessons. My students worked on *"En Aquel Prado"* ("Over in the Meadow"). As part of our studies, we sang the song, constructed a stand-up mural with real props, and with them, dramatized the various animals. The children caught on quickly to the richness of the vocabulary in the book. It was easy, since Spanish is their first language.

For ESL, I introduced and read Ezra Jack Keats' book, *Over in the Meadow*. We sang the words from the book in English, drew and collected the props for the stand-up mural, and dramatized the story again (this version had different animals). The students picked up the vocabulary, read the song in English, and had no trouble understanding the work since a very similar version had already been covered in Spanish.

The crowning moment came when one of my students shared his drawing of a lizard lying in the sun and said, "Look, Mrs. Rosenberg, he's basking in the sun." Wow! Not bad for a kindergartner who entered school speaking no English!

Stefani Rosenberg
Ninth Street School
Los Angeles, California

S H O P T A L K

Peyton, Joy Kreeft and Leslee Reed. *Dialogue Journal Writing with Nonnative English Speakers: A Handbook for Teachers.* Alexandria, Virginia: TESOL, 1990.

It's common these days for teachers to have their second language learners do some sort of journal writing. If we're not careful, though, journal writing can easily become "compliance" writing, with students making journal entries in response to teacher-assigned topics. And "interactive" journals can easily become a one-way street, with students doing nearly all the writing, and the teacher writing only tiny comments in the margins, checking rather than responding to entries. Students quickly learn that the teacher is a lot more interested in how much they're writing than in what they're writing about. Peyton and Reed's terrific little book focuses on using journals for authentic, two-way, learner-centered communication. You'll find all the information you need to get written student-teacher conversations underway and to keep them going strong throughout the school year. The book is packed with student samples that illustrate the power of dialogue journals in developing literacy skills for students at all stages of English language proficiency. Especially valuable are the authors' helpful hints on overcoming the typical obstacles associated with dialogue journals— dealing with reluctant, repetitive, and blocked writers.

The whole mix falls under the ever-expanding Natural Approach umbrella. Each strategy and technique helps make our teaching, and therefore the academic content of school, easier to understand for second language learners. Equally important, each helps keep the focus on using a second language (or first language, for that matter) for meaningful, natural communication.

Like any area of education, second language acquisition theory is evolutionary in nature. Nothing with second language learner instruction therefore, is ever set in concrete. Theories and practices change as new ideas and approaches are proposed and tested out in classrooms. And at any given point, theorists can vigorously disagree with one another, each marshalling a large set of studies to support his or her own set of assumptions about how a second language is—or should be—developed. For example, many of Stephen Krashen's notions, such as his downplaying of the role of conscious learning and grammar study in second language teaching, continue to be hotly contested by people like Barry McLaughlin (McLaughlin 1990) and Christopher Brumfit (Brumfit 1992). Where does this leave teachers who, after all, must walk into the classroom tomorrow and help their second language learners get hold of content and English? No teacher has the luxury of time to wait until the dust settles to see how the latest theory battle is resolved. What teachers can do, however, is operate from a clearly defined theoretical base, modifying that base and adopting new strategies when their journal reading, reflection, and experience show that the new strategies increase learning for second language students.

Field Notes: Teacher-To-Teacher

I've noticed that when it comes to language acquisition, children learn what they need. Learning a second language has a lot to do with the individual initiative of each child. Last year I had a pair of twins, José and Sandra. Both started the year as non-English speakers. José is very outgoing, likes to be a leader, and soon made many friends among both English and Spanish speakers. Toward the end of the year, José tried to communicate with me exclusively in English, only using Spanish when he was unable to get his point across in English. On the other hand, Sandra is a timid child who seldom speaks unless adults address her first. She chose her playmates from among the other Spanish-speaking children in class. I never heard her trying to speak English on her own, though she participated in the shared reading in English and sang along with all the English songs. I was happy when both twins showed progress on the Language Assessment Standardized test. Sandra scored ten points higher, José, thirty points. Sandra learned the English she needed to participate in classroom activities. José learned more because his goal was to be a classroom leader.

Laurel Cress
Longfellow School
Hayward, California

S H O P T A L K

Krashen, Stephen D. and Tracy D. Terrell *The Natural Approach: Language Acquisition in the Classroom.* Englewood Cliffs, New Jersey: Alemany Press, 1983.

Here's the book that helped revolutionize second language teaching. Today, its clear explanations still help teachers understand the theory and research behind communication-based methodology. More importantly, the book's detailed activity examples assist teachers in implementing the Natural Approach in the classroom. A "must read."

Stages of Language Acquisition

Research in language acquisition (Brown 1973; Pinker 1994) has shown that people of all ages pass through identifiable stages of development as they acquire both first and second languages. (See chart on page 54.) Knowing the characteristics of each stage—Pre-Production, Early Production, Speech Emergence, Intermediate Fluency, and Native Level Fluency/Proficiency—can help us plan developmentally appropriate activities for students.

Kids, of course, don't walk into the classroom with one of the stage names printed neatly across their foreheads. And that's as it should be, since there's often overlap in the stages. A student can be mostly at Stage 2, for example, yet have an element of what's primarily associated with Stage 3. The stages simply serve as general signposts along a fluid developmental highway.

Following are three important points to remember about the stages:

- low proficiency does not equal low ability
- critical thinking should happen at all stages
- literacy building should happen at all stages.

Looking at Language Proficiency—
Conversational and Academic Language

Without broad-based assessment, including careful observation and reflection, teachers can easily think second language learners have a lot less or a lot more English than they really have.

Overreliance on single-source assessment may lead a teacher to underestimate a student's second language skills. Some standardized language proficiency instruments, for example, are infamous for catching kids on the language they don't know rather than on what they do know.

Language Acquisition Stages

Stage 1: Pre-Production

- minimal comprehension
- no verbal production

Receptive to English when

- listening
- matching
- pointing
- miming
- moving
- choosing
- drawing
- role-playing silently

Stage 2: Early Production

- limited comprehension
- minimal verbal production

Receptive to and expressive with English when

- naming
- labeling
- listing
- categorizing
- responding with one or two words

Stage 3: Speech Emergence

- good comprehension
- many pronunciation and grammatical errors
- produces simple sentences (with limited descriptive vocabulary)

Receptive to and expressive with English when

- describing
- retelling
- defining
- summarizing
- explaining
- comparing and contrasting

Stage 4: Intermediate Fluency

- excellent comprehension
- near-native speech
- few pronunciation and grammatical errors

Receptive to and expressive with English when

- giving opinions
- analyzing
- synthesizing
- debating
- evaluating
- justifying
- examining
- reading
- writing

Stage 5: Native Level Fluency/Proficiency

Stage blocks originally developed by Connie Williams and Stephen Cary, based on Terrell (1981).

Underestimating second language skills may result in low teacher expectations, nonengaging school work, and student boredom.

Overestimating second language skills is just as possible—and just as serious in its consequences. Fluency in oral, face-to-face communications is sometimes mistakenly seen as an indicator of overall proficiency in a second language. A fourth-grade second language student who speaks fluidly and effectively in English with her classmates, however, may lack English literacy skills and familiarity with the language of mathematics, science, and history. Overestimating second language skills may lead to unrealistically high teacher expectations, undoable school work, loss of self-esteem, and premature exit from a bilingual program.

Avoiding under- and overestimates of second language strength is tricky business. Looking at language in terms of proficiency "types" can help. Some theorists and researchers draw a distinction between conversational and academic language proficiency (Skutnabb-Kangas and Toukomaa 1976; Snow et al. 1991; Cummins 1996). Cummins (1980) originally used the terms BICS (Basic Interpersonal Communication Skills) and CALP (Cognitive Academic Language Proficiency) for describing two "faces" of language proficiency. In the dual-face model, conversational language, or surface fluency, is what students need for social situations like the school playground. Academic language, which includes reading and writing, is what students need for the heavier cognitive and content demands of school.

At the heart of the conversational-academic distinction is the degree to which the meaning in a communication is supported or contextualized. Conversational language is contextualized with a variety of clues—the immediate setting, objects, facial expressions, movement, intonation, question-answer trades, instant feedback—that help second language learners make meaning out of what's being said. Academic language, on the other hand, is decontextualized. Reading a chapter book, locating information online or in a science text, solving a math word problem, understanding a debate, or writing a short story, must all be done without interpersonal cues. Meaning-making in these activities depends on skill in interpreting linguistic cues, using only language itself to figure out what the language is saying. Moreover, compared to face-to-face conversations, academic activities can require the processing of much larger amounts of information. As the grades roll by, school becomes less concrete (fewer manipulatives, models, and visuals are used) and more abstract, more decontextualized, with an accompanying demand for higher level reading and writing skills. Without academic language and especially strong literacy skills, second language learners have little chance of succeeding in school.

The dual-face language proficiency model, however, remains controversial. Its critics (Edelsky et al. 1983; Frederickson and Cline 1990) see the conversational-academic distinction as vague and hypothetical, and an over-simplification of complex language processes. In the real world of second language acquisition, there's no border neatly dividing Conversation Land from Academic Land. And always associating cognitively undemanding communication with conversational English, and cognitively demanding communication with academic English, may cause teachers to misjudge how difficult certain activities are. For example, it may be tempting, at first glance, to see a short, improvised role-play with props and costumes as a "no-sweat," "low-think" activity for beginning-level second language learners. After all, here's a conversational setting with lots of meaning-making contextual clues in place. Contextual supports, however, regardless of how helpful they may be, won't turn the role play into a completely smooth and effortless endeavor on the language/thinking front. Even a short conversation on a familiar topic can be a linguistically complex, cognitively "heavy" task for a student with beginning-level English proficiency. And longer conversations can be especially challenging and exhausting, both mentally and physically.

	Conversational Language (BICS)	**Academic Language (CALP)**
What	social language, playground talk, basic oral skills	academic language, classroom talk, oral and literacy skills
Needed for	making friends, meeting basic needs, basic comprehension	academic success, career options
Developed through	interaction with native speakers and comprehensible teaching activities	interaction with native speakers and comprehensible teaching activities, plus comprehensible literacy activities
Variables	motivation, self-esteem level, home support, emotional health, sociability	motivation, self-esteem level, home support, emotional health, sociability, plus degree of first language literacy
Acquisition stage	1-2-3	4-5
Time needed to develop	two to three years depending on the influences and variables such as those above	three to four years depending on the influences and variables above

Please note: • Total time stages 1-5 = five to seven years
• See page 55 for caveat on the conversational-academic distinction

Clearly, students need both BICS and CALP, and the way they obtain them is through lots of opportunities to use both in meaningful ways in low-stress environments. It's the Magic 7 all over again.

Importance of the Students' Primary Language

As you may recall from Chapter 1, studies have shown repeatedly that second language learners who develop a strong oral and written foundation in their primary language have more success in school than children with weak first language skills. Current research studies by David Ramirez (1991), Virginia Collier (1992), and W. P. Thomas and Collier (1995) continue to support primary language program models.

Anything teachers can do to support and develop students' primary language will help them learn English, subject area content, and in turn, help students feel good about themselves as learners. In the context of bilingual education,

- *support* refers to sporadic, short-term help in students' primary language
- *development* refers to consistent, long-term help, and includes building students' primary language literacy skills.

We can support students' primary language throughout the day in all kinds of learning situations. For example, notice how Wayne Lindse supports and values his students' bilingual skills in this interactive math journal.

Clearly, students need both BICS and CALP, and the way they obtain them is through lots of opportunities to use both in meaningful ways in low-stress environments.

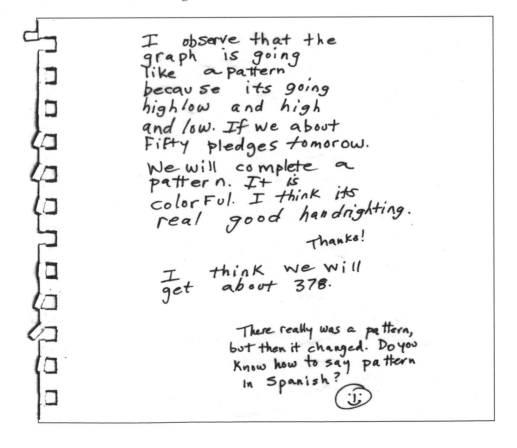

Field Notes: Teacher-To-Teacher

I want my students to know that I value their primary language—Spanish. So I spent two summers attending an immersion language institute in Mexico and learned to speak Spanish. My Spanish is far from perfect, but both my students and their parents are delighted—and grateful—that I can converse with them in their native tongue. They never criticize my Spanish; indeed, they applaud all my attempts and help me in every way they can. To create a rich, literate environment in my classroom, I've also made sure to include materials in both English and Spanish. I've labeled many of the items in our classroom (chalkboard, library, window, and so forth) so children will have literacy references as they are learning to read and write. I include written samples in Spanish and English, and I've filled the room with children's literature in both languages. In all these ways, my children know that I value their language—which means that I value them.

Etty Korengold
Fair Oaks School
Redwood City, California

Carefully structured, long-term maintenance bilingual programs produce proficient bilingual and biliterate students. These programs are "additive" in nature. They develop and maintain the first language while adding on a second, in contrast to "subtractive" programs that replace the first language with the second. Bilingual teachers help second language learners build English skills and, at the same time, give students immediate, full, and sustained access to the core curriculum through first language instruction.

But I don't speak Vietnamese! The shortage of credentialed bilingual teachers prevents many schools from setting up comprehensive, grade-extended bilingual programs. Moreover, the vast majority of schools fortunate enough to have bilingual staff usually offer an English-Spanish program. Programs serving other language groups such as Cantonese, Vietnamese, and Navajo exist, but they are few and far between.

So there you are, along with hundreds of other teachers in the same boat—at a school with no bilingual program (or a minimal one), in a classroom with anywhere from two to a half-dozen different primary languages, excited to be working with your own little United Nations, knowing the critical nature of first language skills, and wanting very much to support your students' primary languages. But you're not bilingual, much less multilingual.

All is not lost. You can still support kids' primary language and in so doing, support their content learning and English acquisition. The "Supporting Students' Primary Language" summary on pages 60-64 offers a summary of supports.

Change the message to parents. For years, well-meaning teachers and administrators told parents of second language learners to downplay their native tongue and instead, use as much English as they could with their children. The problem was that some parents didn't have much English to use; others didn't have any. Parents often left school meetings confused

Field Notes: Teacher-To-Teacher

How can you increase primary language support in your classroom if you don't speak your students' primary languages? There are lots of ways. Here are some ideas:

- Build a classroom library of books in languages other than English. This is essential for primary language development. You may want to pool your resources with colleagues.

- Encourage journal writing in your students' first languages. A bilingual aide or parent volunteer can read and respond to the entries.

- To increase the primary language resources in classrooms, publish stories in your writer's workshop in languages other than English. Invite your bilingual students to share their stories with their classmates.

- Look around the classroom at your environmental print. Include signs in your students' primary languages, as well as articles and stories in English about the students' countries of origin.

- Invite second language students to participate in show and tell using their first languages. They can explain objects or events from their homelands.

Yvonne and David Freeman
Fresno Pacific College
Fresno, California

and feeling guilty about speaking their own language to their children. Times have changed, I'm happy to report. At a recent parent advisory council meeting in a district north of San Francisco that I attended, the superintendent encouraged Latino parents to take time to talk with their kids, tell them stories, and read to them as often as they could in the language the parents knew best—Spanish.

Change the message to students. Before the late 60s, Latino children in California and throughout the Southwest were often punished for speaking Spanish at school. The punishment was usually the privilege withdrawal type, but sometimes it was corporal. Regardless of its form, the punishment sent a signal to kids that was loud and clear: your native language—and by logical extension, your native culture—is unsuitable. Needless to say, this was not the American school system's finest hour in self-esteem building. That hour, unfortunately, stretched out a bit—at least in one classroom. As recently as 1988, the *San Francisco Chronicle* reports, a California high school teacher was fining his Asian immigrant students a dime any time they strayed from his English-only policy.

Supporting Students' Primary Language

Bilingual Instructional Aide

Advantages

- A bilingual aide can interpret and translate for students.
- An aide can preview and review new, tough concepts.
- An aide can help with first language literacy development, make appropriate use of first language materials, and serve as a bridge to parents of second language learners.

Considerations

- You'll need time together to plan and coordinate.
- Volunteers will need initial and ongoing training.
- Avoid concurrent translation. Kids may tune out English if a first language translation always follows on its heels.

Bilingual Parent Volunteer

Advantages

- The parent can offer first language interpreting and translating.
- The parent has an opportunity to learn more about how school works.
- The children see the parent involved, caring, and concerned.
- The parent has the chance to share something of his or her work and culture (oral history, folktale, dance, cuisine, and so on).

Considerations

- The parent's help may be infrequent and short-term.
- The willing parent may not know teacher's preferred way of helping.

Bilingual University Student Volunteer

Advantages

- The university volunteer can interpret and translate for students.
- The volunteer may be the only other person at the school who speaks a particular student's first language.
- The volunteer can serve as a "big brother or sister," providing younger students with emotional support.

Considerations

- The student may provide infrequent, short-term help.
- The student may need training on how to help.

Bilingual Student Buddy

Advantages

- The bilingual buddy can interpret and translate for students.
- The buddy can provide ongoing help.
- The buddy can sometimes "get through" when a teacher can't.
- Buddies build their own self-esteem as their bilingual skills are valued.

Considerations

- The "chemistry" between a bilingual buddy and a second language learner needs to be right.
- The buddy may need modeling to learn how to help and how not to help.
- The buddy can experience burnout if asked to help too much. You may need to rotate buddy jobs.
- Helping should be a two-way street: the student getting help needs to give help at other times to maintain his or her self-esteem.

Bilingual Cross-age Tutor

Advantages

- A cross-age tutor can interpret and translate for students.
- A tutor can serve as a "big brother" or "big sister," providing emotional support.

- A tutor is available right on site.
- A tutor can gain as much academically as a tutored student.

Considerations

- Tutors may need initial training.
- Tutors may miss learning opportunities in their own classrooms while they're tutoring.

Parents Encourage Development of the First Language at Home

Advantages

- Parents help children build a strong foundation in their first language.
- Parents feel that their first language and home culture are valued.

Considerations

- Parents may need ideas and materials to support their children's primary language.
- Parents may be nonliterate or semiliterate in their first language. They may therefore need information on the ways they can help their children develop first language literacy.
- Parents may understand the need for using their native language at home but not at school. They may therefore need information on the rationale for bilingual education.

Teacher Works To Become Bilingual

Advantages

- Having even a little knowledge of students' first language can be helpful to them and to you.
- Learning students' first language tells them that you value their language and you value them.

Consideration

- Becoming bilingual will take time!

Primary Language is Incorporated into the Regular School Day

Possibilities include a poem in Vietnamese, a song in Tagalog, a jump-rope rhyme in Lao, a character in a play speaking Hmong, or counting off in Spanish.

Advantages

- Using students' first language tells them that you value their language and you value them.
- Students speaking only English get to learn a little of a second language.
- Kids can take the lead in teaching the activity.

Considerations

- It's important to include all languages represented in the class.
- You'll need some time to explore the possibilities and gather materials to contextualize activities.

Commercial First Language Material

Advantages

- First language material, such as parallel texts, trade books, reference materials, videos and CD-ROMs can provide access to the core curriculum.
- Older students who are literate in their first language, can sometimes work independently with the material or with minimal teacher/aide direction.

Considerations

- Most students will need a bilingual teacher, aide, or volunteer to help them effectively use first language materials.
- Staff fluent in the first language should review the material.
- The availability of material in languages other than Spanish is limited but slowly improving.

Teacher- and Student-Created First Language Material

Advantages

- Material such as summaries of literature, original stories, poems, songs, correspondence, class newspapers, and class anthologies can be tailor-made to fit the immediate needs of kids.
- Students improve their literacy and research skills as they develop first language material.

Considerations

- Developing good material takes time.
- With summaries, some meaning from the original text will be lost.

Before- and After-School Primary Language Programs

Advantages

- Program staff can interpret and translate for students.
- The program can provide consistent, possibly long-term support and development for children's first language.
- The program can offer native English-speaking students second language opportunities.

Considerations

- Adding a program and staff can be expensive.
- Parents whose children are enrolled in the program may experience child-care and transportation problems.
- Care must be taken to ensure connections between the regular school and before- and after-school curriculums.
- The program should never be considered an appropriate substitute for a regular day, comprehensive bilingual program.

S H O P T A L K

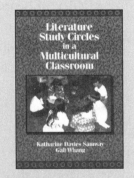

Samway, Katharine Davies and Gail Whang. *Literature Study Circles in a Multicultural Classroom.* York, Maine: Stenhouse Publishers, 1996.

Samway and Whang's thoroughly practical book appeals to all teachers who want to use literature as a learning tool, particularly teachers of multilingual students. Gail Whang teaches fifth-sixth grade in an inner-city Oakland school. She found that her second language learners were becoming bored and discouraged with her language arts program. As a result, she began exploring literature study circles as a way to engage her students in deeply thoughtful conversations about issues and events in their lives. Whang and Samway explain how to create a learner-centered classroom, motivate students, help students become confident readers and thinkers, and keep track of students' reading and responses. In addition, the authors provide bibliographies of popular fifth-sixth grade literature, lists of African American, Asian American, Native American, and Latino authors, and professional readings on literature study circles.

Chapter 4

Instructional Supports

Let's see where we are. We've

- reviewed program models for second language learners
- outlined the basics of effective second language learner instruction
- talked a little theory, paying particular attention to the critical need for supporting and developing students' primary language.

Now, let's take a closer look at specific strategies and techniques that help students with second language acquisition and content learning.

Make Instruction Concrete

If you want to throw second language learners for a major loop, especially students brand new to English, stand up in front of them and talk. Just talk. A large portion of all those words streaming out of your mouth—and the concepts they attempt to convey—will fly right over the heads of second language kids. Unless we provide a context and plenty of context clues connecting words to objects, visuals, and movements, our language remains fuzzy and abstract. Contextualized instruction that expands the literacy spectrum is concrete, meaningful, comprehensible, engaging, and effective.

Keeping instruction concrete with context clues. Let's imagine that during a third-grade theme cycle on the environment, students become interested in species preservation. Small groups research and report on various threatened and endangered animals around the world. One group has fired up the entire class about alligators and crocodiles. Students pose a couple dozen questions regarding crocodilians.

- Did alligators ever live in California?
- Where are crocodile farms located?
- Who sells crocodile products at the local mall?
- How much do poachers make per hide?
- What laws protect crocodiles?
- How many babies do alligators have?
- Do alligators see colors?
- Can you really hold a crocodile's jaw shut?
- How much land and water does one alligator need to survive?
- What can the class do to help preserve crocodiles?

Their questions are then pared down, with similar ones grouped together in categories such as distribution, efforts to save, behavior, and life cycle. In a mix of individual, pair, and small group work, students pursue answers to their questions.

The teacher, with the help of students, is careful to provide a wide array of context clues (video clips, crocodilian teeth, anatomy diagram, species distribution map, poacher data graph) and access to students' multiple intelligences, so that the activities stay concrete and easy to understand.

Keeping instruction concrete with Total Physical Response. For about twenty-five years, teachers of second language learners have been using James Asher's (1969, 1977, 1982) Total Physical Response (TPR) method. With TPR, students respond physically to commands, manipulate objects, and are allowed a lengthy silent period before producing language. Almost all kids find the method intrinsically fun and engaging. Students break from the sit-and-listen mode and are active and psychologically safe since speaking is never forced. The method has helped large numbers of second language learners acquire English.

TPR, however, can easily turn into meaningless drill if we're not careful. For example: "Luz, pick up the book; put the book under the table; put the book on your head; open the book; close the book; give the book to Gloria; Gloria, pick up the book." I don't know about Luz or Gloria, but after about ten minutes of this stuff, I'd want to hide the book!

As it turns out, there *is* life after basic TPR. Because responding to spoken directions for physical tasks keeps instruction concrete, more and more teachers are discovering that within the context of meaningful activities, TPR helps second language students learn and retain curriculum concepts.

For example, you can move beyond standard TPR and integrate physical response with math and social studies. Rather than starting with a text and illustrations, written explanations, and exercises, introduce your class to the concept of *perimeter* and *town* through a floor activity.

1. With your students, push back all the desks and block out a large rectangle on the classroom floor with string and tape. The rectangle becomes a map of a typical small town. The string perimeter is the town's city limits. Label the map with the key directions. Place photos, drawings, and objects to represent major landmarks.

2. Two students use their imaginations to take you and a couple of their classmates on a walking tour of the town.

3. Suggest to students that they measure the length around the town. One student, Elena, offers her foot as a measuring device.

4. Several students get a sense of one Elena-size foot by running a finger along the bottom of Elena's shoe.

5. Students estimate the number of Elena feet (heel to toe) around the string perimeter. After you record and graph the estimates on large chart paper, students determine the range of guesses, low to high (twenty-two Elena feet to eighty-six Elena feet, for example).

6. Elena walks the perimeter and everybody's estimates (even yours) are compared with the actual length in Elena feet.

7. Other students walk the perimeter, then compare their foot sizes to Elena's and to standard meter or yardstick measurements.

8. Students divide into small groups and construct smaller rectangles (mini-towns or villages) per your measurement directions (for example, 4'2" by 5'7"). More estimating, recording, and graphing follow.

Throughout the floor activity, Elena and other students respond to the wealth of informal, naturally occurring Total Physical Response commands. These verbal directions are meaningful and enable students to develop their second language as they learn math and social studies. In math, for example, students learn what quadrants are when they divide the rectangle with different colored string. They learn area when they estimate how many square feet it takes to fill up each quadrant. And students see that there are different ways to look at lines—through a number line, parallel lines, intersection, and range. In social studies they learn the characteristics of a town, village, city limits, market, mall, and so on.

In this activity, unlike drill-and-kill TPR, the commands are meaningful and do double duty—developing language and helping with content learning.

The TPR statements students might respond to in this activity include:

- Cut the string.
- Please hold the tape for me.
- Place your right toe next to your left heel.
- Walk two steps south, then go east to the market.
- Walk the perimeter/city limits.
- Move your finger along Elena's shoe.
- Write your estimate on the chart paper.
- Draw the town.

A Thematic Instruction Route

Over the past ten to fifteen years, hundreds of teachers have abandoned "subject island" teaching for thematic, inquiry-based instruction. Findings from brain research (Hart 1983) provided an impetus for the switch. Just like adults, children learn by pattern-making, and come equipped with an extraordinary, built-in pattern maker—the brain.

Teaching reading at 8:35 a.m., math at 9:20 a.m., spelling at 10:25 a.m., social studies at 1:00 p.m., and science at 2:05 p.m. didn't lend itself to pattern-making. It was hard for kids (and teachers) to make sense of school and the world, to see a connection between subjects. And for good reason—there usually *was* no attempt to make the connection.

Thematic instruction is a whole new ball game. Kids make connections because teachers explicitly arrange school to help kids make those connections.

Students working on a theme of community, for example, might

- learn a welcome song such as the Liberian "Funga Alafia"
- survey their classmates on their favorite foods, places to go, and things to do, then chart their findings
- observe and draw an ant colony showing the behaviors of the ant community
- work with other classes to create a school collage, complete with pictures, drawings, and writings illustrating their own school community.

With thematic instruction, concepts "flow and grow" throughout the curriculum. The concept of averaging, for example, is no longer confined to a place called "math time." Students trying to answer their questions about how musical instruments work might average the length of notes produced by various xylophone key materials. Later in the week, they present "concerts" in small groups on homemade instruments, then average the audience's reaction using a five-point scale.

What's the big idea? Once students understand the theme or big idea, they can relate what they know and what they find out, in many subjects, back to the theme and back to their own lives. For example, if the class theme is exploration, your students can use their prior knowledge of personal exploration to first understand the concept and then learn more about it through content curriculum. You might begin the theme with a read-aloud of Dr. Seuss's *Oh, The Places You'll Go!* to help them visualize exploration. Then, invite children to think about an adventure they've had. Perhaps they learned how to do something new or found their own special place. You might also want to share an exploration of your own. Children can create a picture memory map, using different colors and shapes to depict their journey, then make a word map about their meaningful experiences. Students can further study exploration in history, finding out how different groups first came to America; in science, exploring technological advances, how inventors think of new ideas and ways of doing things, and making some of their own inventions; in math, how explorers find their way to new places using maps; how authors explore ways of writing stories through many drafts; and how to express these adventures through music, dance, and drama. Using a theme or big idea enables students to make connections and deepen their understandings.

Depth and breadth. Students can't help but be engaged in the study and have a sense of ownership over their learning when we begin with questions and issues that interest them. As they research answers to their questions, students become experts in their area of study, and in turn, enhance their self-esteem.

Access for all students. Theme-centered inquiry provides a welcoming and challenging curriculum for all students, regardless of ability, developmental language proficiency, or skill level. Students learn to work and solve problems individually and with a group, discovering that they can learn from each other.

Thematic instruction helps all students—including second language learners—make greater sense of content, and there are added advantages for students learning a second language. Because thematic instruction is high interest, interactive, and context-rich, it allows students to

- take risks for learning language. Risk-taking comes naturally when kids are interested, engaged learners who feel safe and supported.
- make friends and acclimate to a new country and community faster. Collaboration invites lots of conversation and often leads to new friendships.

- serve as home culture experts and raise self-esteem. Students become the resident experts when an area of study touches upon their cultural and linguistic background.
- learn language and content. Students acquire language as they use it to learn relevant, engaging content.

A How-To Framework for Thematic Instruction

Thematic instruction comes in all shapes and sizes. Talk with ten teachers and you'll find ten different ways to go about it. For teachers new to thematic instruction or veteran folks looking for new twists in the road, here's a suggested framework known as a *theme cycle*.

Field Notes: Teacher-To-Teacher

After learning about the characteristics of fish and the process of weighing and cleaning them, our class held a "Fish Feast." Two parents with different ethnic traditions came to school and prepared fish. A mother from Puerto Rico cooked *Bacalau*, a fried fish served with tomato sauce, and an African American parent showed us how to make breaded, Southern-style fish. What a delicious way to extend our learning about fish and celebrate the many backgrounds and traditions in our class!

Amika Kemmler Ernst
Blackstone Elementary School
Boston, Massachusetts

Choose a theme. There are many ways to choose a theme or topic of study. You'll want to field ideas from your students and negotiate a choice together. Here are points to consider:

- Thematic "spark" can come from you and/or your students.
- Choose a topic with potential for in-depth research and content integration.
- Honor students' real interests and questions.
- The content areas serve the theme instead of the theme serving the content areas. For example, as students do a crocodilian theme, they acquire knowledge about biological taxonomy and how ecosystems work. They also hone their hypothesizing, observing, and data recording and

analysis skills. But, first and foremost, kids want to pursue alligators and crocodiles to learn about alligators and crocodiles—not to learn science skills.

Assess knowledge base and interest level and organize curriculum. Next, you'll want to determine what students know about the chosen theme and what they want and need to learn. With that information, you can plan your instruction accordingly.

- Brainstorm with students what they know and what they want to know—this will serve as an informal assessment.

- As students pose questions about the theme, also pose questions yourself. Modeling the "spirit of inquiry" will show kids you want to learn right along with them.

- Sort and categorize the questions. One way to know if the theme has learning potential is to look at the number of questions raised. When students are genuinely interested in pursuing a topic, they'll be enthusiastically raising dozens of hands and questions. Few questions and those posed halfheartedly indicate a need to switch themes.

Field Notes: Teacher-To-Teacher

Keeping writing notebooks encourages kids in all stages of writing proficiency to think, create, and make personal connections to the text they are reading. Writing notebooks prompt students to jot down notes, draw symbols and pictures, and copy sections of a text they find interesting. The collection of these thoughts, musings, sketches, and favorite quotes becomes, to our writers, a rich source for writing, just as an artist's sketch book is a source for a final masterpiece. From their notebooks, students choose an idea to develop into a polished composition. In this way, they come to realize that "I have many wonderful ideas, I enjoy writing, and I can do it well!"

Wendy Motoike
Encinita School
Rosemead, California

- Form research groups based on the questions. Each category can serve as the name of an inquiry group. With the crocodilian theme, you might end up with five groups—Anatomy, Hunting Behavior, Eating Behavior, Distribution, Habitat, and Preservation Efforts.
- Together with your students, determine what activities will help them find answers to their questions.
- Identify the key concepts that you will teach directly.

Gather resources. You'll want your students to understand that they will use many resources, not just an encyclopedia, to find answers to their questions. The resources include

- community resource people, parents, classroom visitors
- online resources
- books, magazines, pamphlets, newspapers
- maps, drawings, photos, artifacts
- slides, films, tapes, CDs, videos, CD-ROMs
- field trips.

Provide direct instruction and modeling. Periodically throughout the theme cycle, you'll want to teach key concepts. You can teach through modeling your own research strategies such as skimming, scanning, and note-taking. Ask students to create mindmaps to quickly assess what they are learning and where they need help.

Provide time for student inquiry. As they come to know about a particular subject, students need time to conduct their research. They also need time to show what they've learned through presentations and research products. Finally, students bring their learning full-cycle when they have time to reflect on what they have learned. Students can

- conduct their inquiries as individuals, with a partner, or in collaborative research groups
- present their research using a variety of formats including an oral report, a video, a play, or through the demonstration of a scientific experiment.

Field Notes: Teacher-To-Teacher

For several years now, my fifth-grade bilingual class has been creating and broadcasting a weekly half-hour radio show. With a $2,000 grant, we were able to purchase basic radio equipment: two CD players, a tape recorder, a mixer, two microphones, two headphones, and jacks. Every Friday morning, students open the show with music, read student-submitted stories and poems, and give a brief news report, including noteworthy events on local, state, and national levels. Students report on sports, make general announcements, conduct interviews (often relating to what we're studying), and broadcast Sensational Citizen Awards—certificates given to students, staff, and community members for service to the school or for academic achievement. Students close with some sort of contest—questions about geography, for instance—and sign off with more music.

By accelerating English acquisition, and providing varied and authentic opportunities for my second language kids to read, write, and speak, our radio show has enhanced bilingual skills. It has also increased multicultural awareness in our school and in our community. All in all, it's proved to be a rewarding, stimulating, and fun way to promote functional language and literacy development. Now, I can't imagine teaching any other way!

Roberta Lee
Fair Oaks School
Redwood City, California

Making Speech Easy To Understand

If you've traveled abroad, chances are good you've found yourself in the following situation. You're at a train station trying to buy a ticket to a city whose name you can't pronounce. Realizing that you're a foreigner (if the botched pronunciation wasn't the tip-off, the Bermuda shorts and dangling camera are), the ticket agent repeats the basic information two or three times. When you still look confused and desperate, he raises his voice for a last try. Even with megaphone-level volume, he's still incomprehensible, and you end up spending the weekend in Bucaramanga instead of Buenaventura.

We know that when we're speaking in a normal volume and aren't getting through, speaking in a louder voice doesn't help. In fact, it can make things worse. In the classroom, gaining proximity to the person we're speaking to and looking them in the eye may help a bit, but not a lot—especially with many of our Southeast Asian kids who avoid direct eye contact with the teacher out of respect.

So how do we talk to second language learners, especially those who are at a beginning English level? Here are some speech modification suggestions. For additional speech support ideas, refer back to "What Effective Teachers Do" in Chapter 2.

Speak at standard speed. If you're a speedy talker (you can name all the state capitals in less than thirty seconds), you may have to put a "governor on the tongue" every so often. Most teachers, however, won't need to alter their typical speaking speed since what we're shooting for is a normal, comfortable rate of speaking. Speech slowed to a turtle's pace becomes artificial; it loses the rhythm and natural flow of the language. However, providing more and slightly longer pauses gives students a little more time to make sense of what you're saying.

Use more gestures, movement, and facial expressions. Talking with your hands and body, and doing a little shameless mugging every now and then adds emphasis to your words and provides extra clues for students to search for meaning. Avoid the deadpan; leave the sphinx face at home.

Be careful with fused forms. Language compressions, for example, "D'yathinkshe'sgonnawannaplaywithimatrecess?" (Do you think she's going to want to play with him at recess?) can be difficult for students new to English. So, do we stop compressing altogether? Probably not. First of all, it's hard not to compress. We all compress now and then, knowhatamean? And second, our students will have to deal with plenty of fused forms both in and out of the classroom. Experienced teachers keep an ear open to their own speech so that they use fused forms without overusing or eliminating them altogether. They let phrases and whole sentences tumble out, sounding like the words were caught in an auto wrecking machine press. Then, they watch for students' puzzled expressions, and repeat the phrase or sentence— this time ironed and stretched out to a more easily understood length.

Field Notes: Teacher-To-Teacher

I once asked a Vietnamese student to "tell another Vietnamese child what I had been saying…" The student turned and repeated in English what I had already been unsuccessful in communicating. It takes time and discussion to help bilingual students learn how to become successful translators.

Carol Wright
William Anderson Elementary
Lawndale, California

Use shorter, simpler sentences. Sometimes, talking in compound-complex sentences can even confuse intermediate-stage second language learners.

For example, we can take a sentence that makes more turns than a UPS truck:

Julie, the main character in *Julie of the Wolves*, is courageous and resourceful, but is just a book character, unlike Trinh, who actually experienced terror and hardship in real life when she made her escape with other family members from Vietnam and entered the U.S. in the late seventies.

and turn it into something that's easier to understand for second language learners:

Julie, the main character in *Julie of the Wolves*, is courageous and resourceful. However, she is just a book character, unlike Trinh, who is a real person. When she escaped from Vietnam, Trinh was terrified and had many difficult times. Other people in her family had hard times too. Trinh and her family entered the U.S. in the late seventies.

Use specific names in place of fuzzy pronouns. A fourth-grade teacher checks on a small group of students who are constructing a model castle. Instead of confusing students by saying, "Let me see what you did here. First she built its back wall, then he added his. Then they built up theirs where they usually stood and fought. Right?" the teacher might say, "Let's see what this group has made. First, Susi built the castle's back wall. Then Victor added the side walls. Then Tinh and Wing Shu built up the front wall, where the archers usually stood and fought the enemy. Right?"

Realistically, chances are none of these speech modifications will make a big difference if used alone and infrequently. Taken together, however, and consistently applied in the classroom, the modifications help make our speech and content easier to understand for second language students.

Reading Supports

How can José do the reading if José can't read? He can't—not without some support in place. And if José is a Stage 1, 2, or 3 student with few literacy skills, he'll need *lots* of support. He may not be able to decode at all in English. If he decodes—that is, says what's on the printed page—he may not understand what he's said. Even at Intermediate Fluency (Stage 4), it's likely that José won't be reading as proficiently as his peers whose primary language is

English. He'll require some extra assistance and alternatives to the standard read-on-your-own route, especially if we want him (and we do!) to feel like a real part of the classroom and have success with grade-level materials.

S H O P T A L K

Johnson, Terry D. and Daphne R. Louis. *Literacy through Literature*. Portsmouth, New Hampshire: Heinemann, 1987.

Teacher Wendy Motoike has this to say about *Literacy through Literature*: "This is a foundational guide for teachers implementing a literature-based approach to language arts. Included are a variety of integrated language arts activities that encourage students to respond creatively to literature through drama, art, journal writing, and creation of charts. What I really like about this book is that it can be used with all my students. Its value for children learning a second language is twofold. First, the activities are interactive and provide a motivating and meaningful focus for developing all language arts skills—listening, speaking, reading, and writing. Second, when second language students are included in learning with their English-speaking peers, they feel part of the classroom community and see that we value their contributions."

Primary language parallel material. To provide background in the content, second language learners are provided a primary language version of the text or trade book.

Oral or written summary in the primary language. The bilingual teacher, aide, or bilingual peer provides a periodic summary of material in the primary language.

Oral or written summary in the second language. The teacher, aide, or peer provides second language learners with a periodic summary of material in English, boiling a text chapter or story down to its crucial points. The downside of this approach and the first language summarizing route is obvious: Especially if provided by a student, the summary may leave out a number of important items. Sometimes students understand parts of a main story or text, but not the whole of it. And it's easy to overdo the use of peer tutors. Helpers may feel unreasonably burdened if consistently asked to provide summaries. Second language summarizing also assumes the student has enough English to understand the summary. There *are* some potential problems with summaries, but they're still better than providing no support at all.

Field Notes: Teacher-To-Teacher

I'm about as pro-video in the classroom as a person can get, but I haven't always been. As a new teacher some years back, I steered clear of films and videos. I'd show one every couple months at the most. I figured kids were watching enough TV at home, and I was also worried that I might turn into another Mr. Sprockets.

Mr. Sprockets, as we affectionately referred to him in the teacher's lounge, was a veteran teacher who would walk in at the beginning of each school week weighted down with at least a dozen film canisters from the local County Office of Education. The running joke was that Mr. Sprockets didn't teach—he showed movies. And because movies couldn't teach, or so I believed at that point, kids in my classroom went mostly without movies for several years.

My turnaround came gradually. The more second language kids I worked with, the more I realized how visually dependent they were during English activities. Without something to get their hands and eyes on, they were often lost. Words hooked to visuals carried additional meaning for the kids, and visuals that moved carried even greater meaning.

If you shortchange second language learners and me on paper, pencils, or textbooks, we'll survive; but don't take away that VCR, monitor, computer, and ever-expanding library of video and CD-ROM titles! I like to think Mr. Sprockets would be proud of me.

–SC

Film, video, and CD-ROM. Shown before, in conjunction with, or after the reading, moving pictures will help students better understand the text. Though you won't find a visual counterpart for every piece of literature you and your students want to read, you'll find a lot, sometimes in the students' primary language. Video clips from *National Geographic, Nature, Nova,* and other

PBS shows are potential context-makers for a host of social studies and science activities. If the narration is too hard for students to understand, turn it off and provide your own.

The number of CD-ROM titles is expanding at a staggering rate. CD-ROMs' interactive nature—the mix of text, audio, still, and moving images, its wide curriculum coverage, and especially its ease and speed of use—is quickly making it the visual support material of choice among many teachers who have access to this resource.

S H O P T A L K

Stempleski, Susan and Paul Arcario, eds. *Video in Second Language Teaching*: *Using, Selecting, and Producing Video for the Classroom.* Alexandria, Virginia: TESOL, 1992.

Dust off that VCR and camcorder! Both new and veteran video users will find a wealth of helpful ideas here. Twelve video specialists offer in-depth coverage on videos and young children, video and thematic instruction, language assessment via video, student-produced videos, and choosing and using commercial videos. The book gives teachers the means to move from traditional ESL videos (where the focus is on using videos to teach English) to authentic, high-interest, content-based videos that promote the use of English for real oral and written communication.

Stempleski and Arcario include numerous video previewing, viewing, and postviewing activities applicable across the grades, with an extensive bibliography of additional readings and resources. The editors are the founding members of TESOL (Teachers of English to Speakers of Other Languages) Video Interest Section. The Video Interest Section is one of about twenty TESOL interest groups. Articles from different groups appear regularly in the newsletter, *TESOL Matters.*

Partner reading. There are a number of ways students can help each other do the reading. Here are four of them.

1. A second language learner is paired with a monolingual English speaker who reads the material out loud. The second language student follows along and reads out loud when he or she can.
2. A bilingual student reads to a second language learner in English, offering periodic clarification in the student's primary language. The reader might be a classmate or a cross-age tutor.

3. Student pairs come together and do the reading on a want-to-read basis. This arrangement fits comfortably into a literature studies setting where five or six students with varying first and second language reading proficiencies have all chosen to read a particular book based on a book talk given by the teacher or a student.

4. You or a proficient student reader tapes a story, article, or poem. A second language student listens to the tape and follows along with the text.

Reading Supports that Build Context

Here are some additional tips and techniques for helping all students make more sense of reading material. Some tips use a student's prior knowledge as a bridge into the material. All of them help make reading less abstract by building context.

Tell the story before reading the story. Before a read-aloud of *Toad Is the Uncle of Heaven*, a Vietnamese folktale by Jeanne Lee, bring the children together in a semicircle on the rug, and tell the story using a variety of props, sound effects, and visuals. Invite a few second language learners at Early Production Stage to be "quiet tellers," responding to the story with dramatic action ("Just then, the bees flew in!").

Use mindmaps. After listening to *The Cricket's Pajamas* read aloud, children in a kindergarten-first grade classroom tell their teacher the key elements in the story. The teacher then draws a mindmap to capture their thoughts.

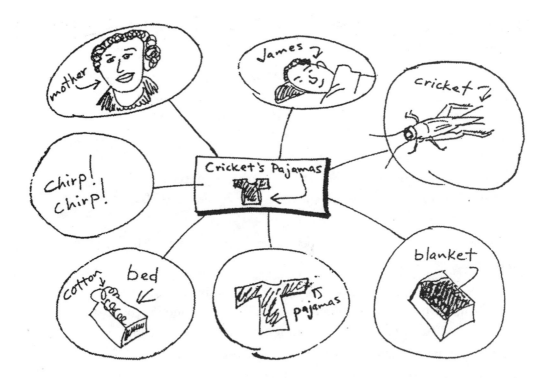

Field Notes: Teacher-To-Teacher

The Reader's Theater is a wonderful tool for learners who are acquiring English literacy skills. I've captured some powerful dialogue from *Charlotte's Web* and rewritten the lines into one-page reader's theaters. Students love reading the piece over and over to get the right mood, intonation, and expression of the characters. Then they perform the piece for the class. Although groups perform the same piece many times, students are "glued" to following the written passage. Who can resist the opening line, "Where's papa going with that ax?"

This is a great way for students to read passages closely and accurately, and to develop comprehension without being overloaded with reading they can't yet handle. In this way, you can use grade- and age-appropriate literature without "insulting" students with easier material geared for very young learners. Later in the school year, students create their own reader's theater from literature used in the classroom.

Lillian Utsumi
Los Angeles Unified School District
Los Angeles, California

Personal student stories. Before reading Jeanette Winter's *Follow the Drinking Gourd* that deals with traveling the Underground Railroad to escape slavery, third grader Blia, a Hmong student, tells her family's story of fleeing Vietnamese soldiers in Laos and the family's eventual escape to safety in Thailand.

Personal teacher stories. After a reading of *The Very Hungry Caterpillar* by Eric Carle, one teacher tells about the time as a little boy when he brought home a caterpillar for a pet, lost it in the living room, then found it living inside his baseball cap a week later.

Quick-talk, quick-write, quick-draw. Students may clip and bring in newspaper and news magazine articles about new environment-friendly inventions. After collecting the articles, redistribute them to pairs of students and ask them to do a two-minute quick-talk followed by a two-minute quick-write or quick-draw. Using only the article titles and visuals, students predict the invention's use, along with how and why it might be good for the environment. Then, after reading and discussing the articles, the pairs report on the accuracy of their predictions.

Field trips. A class of eight, nine, and ten year olds visit a local recycling center and the city landfill before and after doing library research on environmental clean-up proposals. Oral and written language come to life as children experience firsthand the sights, sounds, and smells of the recycling center and landfill. Field trips to a site of study help children build context for their investigation in hands-on, meaningful ways.

Third-grade student Ramón Ramirez, at West Marin School in Pt. Reyes Station, California, made sense of geometric shapes during a walking field trip of his community.

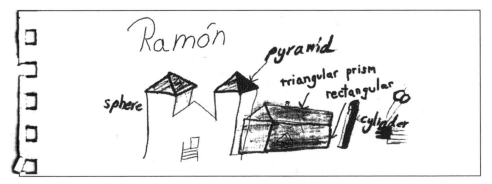

Multilevel reference sets. Let's say your fourth-fifth combination is in the middle of a theme cycle on Traditions. At the start of the cycle, you and some of the students bring in a large reference library—about three dozen books—to be used for ongoing research. The books run the gamut from early primary grade books to college-level texts. As you work with small groups, students see you using and advocating the use of books at all levels. The signal you're sending to all students, especially second language learners, is that any book, regardless of how easy or hard it is to read, is worth consulting if it helps us answer our questions. Without that signal, the fear is that kids will see some of the easier reading level material as "baby stuff." Ironically, however, this material is often the most accessible and helpful for second language students.

Field Notes: Teacher-To-Teacher

I give students self-stick notes to mark pages as they do research. What's marked, depending on the student's reading proficiency, may range from visuals to boldface headings to small passages of text. A second language student may not be able to handle all of the material, or may require additional help or explanations, but is still able to participate in the research process.

Carol Wright
William Anderson Elementary
Lawndale, California

Mapping. Mapping is an instructional technique that helps students learn content and make sense of text through a visual organization of information. Here's a first grader's map of "My Favorite Animals."

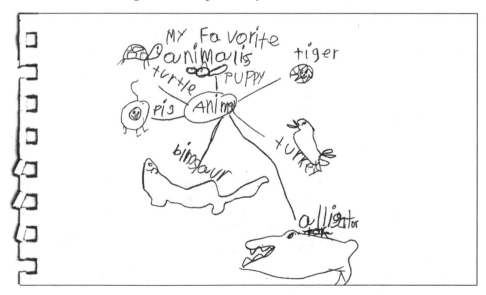

What else do we call it? You might know it as

- mindmapping
- topic mapping
- semantic mapping
- chalk talks
- bubbling
- webbing
- visual brainstorming
- graphic organizing
- clustering
- flow charting.

Granted, there are some differences among these terms. Chalk talks, for example, are associated with quick-sketch drawings that support teacher talk, and semantic mapping is more text-heavy and text-precise than webbing. But regardless of what we call the variations, mapping is a powerful literacy- and content-building technique for all learners.

Mapping, if it's to be really useful, however, has to be more than just words in bubbles. For students with emerging English literacy skills, trying to make sense of reduced text in circles, squares, and triangles is certainly easier than making sense of page after long page of book text. But it's still hard. And if you're a second language learner at square one in your English reading, text in bubbles isn't going to cut it at all, even when the bubbles are color-coded. What will help is reduced text plus visuals—drawings, photos, or cut-out pictures—that bring the bubbled text alive.

Mapping across the curriculum gives students the means to

- construct and see the whole of a multipart lesson
- grasp the interrelationships between characters in a story
- pull out the key ideas in a social studies text
- gain access to high interest, high reading-level reference books
- record a small group's brainstorming ideas
- organize thoughts and feelings for a class discussion
- take nonlinear notes while interviewing.

After reading a chapter of *Julie of the Wolves* to her class, a fifth-grade teacher created this mindmap with support drawings at the overhead. Students shared

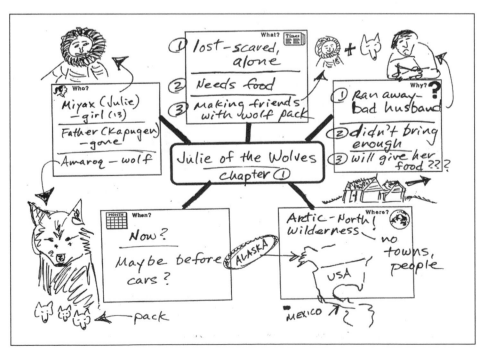

information on the who, what, when, and why of the chapter, then used the map as a base for small group discussion and question posing.

Storyboarding. This is an instructional technique that uses sequenced drawings as a bridge to literacy and an aid for content learning. At Parkside Elementary School in San Mateo, California, third-grade students created storyboards to go with *El Ojo de Dios,* a Native American (Aymará) legend explaining the origin of the colorful yarn and stick art known as God's Eye.

Working in language buddy pairs, students pool their art and language resources to capture and sequence the story's six key plot points. Stanley, who speaks only English, and Vincent, a second language learner, created this storyboard.

Story Board   Name/Group **Stanley/Vincent** Date **10-30**

1. The sun god give the mother 5 chances.

2. She thing the sun god eyes is a wood she can't see sun god eyes.

3. She thing the sun god eyes is a cistay she can't see sungod.

4. And now is the day 5 she cry and cry and is a rainbow

5.

6.

Monica Gomez, from Wayne Lindse's fourth-fifth grade class, created a storyboard to summarize a chapter from the book *Chocolate Fever.*

At Encinita Elementary School in Rosemead, California, Wendy Motoike asks her ESL students to analyze characters by drawing and writing with words and symbols. "I find that this activity is best done during or immediately after an initial reading of a piece of literature to help my students focus their understanding of characters in a story. The storyboard they create serves as a great resource during discussion and for pre-writing." Here's part of sixth grader Edgar Hernandez's character analysis of Snowman, from Phil Mendez's *The Black Snowman.*

To be bona fide, storyboards must have drawings. But how do we get the reluctant drawers drawing? One effective way is to step forward and draw something yourself in front of the kids.

Quick-sketch teacher drawings show students that no one, not even the teacher, has to crank out museum quality art on the storyboards. Kids with art anxiety usually relax, take a crayon or colored pencil in hand, and start drawing along with you.

You might also want to show storyboard samples from other classes with varying levels of drawing expertise. The message to kids is clear: Drawing, like writing, is developmental. It comes in all shapes and sizes and evolves at differing rates. All kids can draw, although you may need to ask some of them to tell you exactly what they've drawn!

Sequenced drawings, with varying amounts of English labeling and text hooked to them, can be applied across the curriculum. Students use them to

- write stories or poems mainly in pictures
- make journal entries of weekend activities
- record key learnings and surprises on a field trip
- capture action points in a literature book chapter
- turn an oral story into a picture book
- block out movements for a play or video production
- give directions for building a circuit board
- document an insect's life cycle
- record weather data for a week
- report steps in a soil treatment experiment
- transform computation problems into a word story problem
- document a typical day in the life of...
- illustrate the steps in constructing a Navajo Hogan.

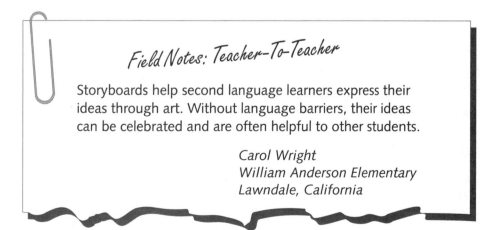

Field Notes: Teacher-To-Teacher

Storyboards help second language learners express their ideas through art. Without language barriers, their ideas can be celebrated and are often helpful to other students.

Carol Wright
William Anderson Elementary
Lawndale, California

Help student presenters prepare material the whole class can see. When students are going to report information to the whole class via mapping or storyboarding, ask them to periodically do their work on overhead transparencies.

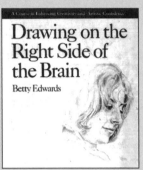

SHOPTALK

Emberley, Ed. *Ed Emberley's Drawing Book of Animals*. New York: Scholastic, 1970.

Edwards, Betty. *Drawing on the Right Side of the Brain*. Los Angeles: Tarcher, 1989.

A few years back, I was convinced I was the world's worst artist. *Ed Emberley's Drawing Book of Animals* and Betty Edwards' *Drawing on the Right Side of the Brain* helped me realize I could really make a horse look like a horse rather than a big dog with long legs. I'm still no great shakes as an artist, but I draw, I enjoy it, and am able to draw in front of kids and teachers now without breaking into a cold sweat. And they even know what I'm drawing most of the time! It's not simply that all kids can draw. All teachers can too!

Drawings done on notebook paper can be seen easily only by the student holding it up and the students sitting immediately in front. Drawings on poster board or butcher paper are usually bigger, but the images on them are often still too small for easy viewing. The overhead projector can enlarge even a small drawing on a transparency and make it big enough so that everyone in the class can enjoy it. One recommendation—the tips of most overhead pens you buy in teacher or office supply stores "mush out" after a short while, sometimes after just a couple of small drawings. Available at art supply stores, Stabilo brand pens come in a variety of colors and tip widths and maintain their points much longer than most other brands, even with the "killer pressing" of first graders. Drawings, charts, maps, poems, and the like, created on plain, unlined paper, can be converted into transparencies in many photocopy machines. Afterward, overhead pens can be used to add color.

Shelter a textbook chapter. Let's imagine. You and your students have created an integrated, inquiry-based curriculum. You use a variety of print material to support students' learning, including tradebooks, magazines, newspapers, multimedia, and student-written materials. Textbooks are used as a program supplement rather than a centerpiece. But you do use them, partly because of the valuable material some of them contain and partly because you're trying to prepare students for the textbook-heavy school years ahead.

How we use materials often determines their effectiveness. Textbooks are no exception. Give most second language learners a "read-the-chapter-answer-the-questions" assignment, and it's lots-of-luck time. Here's one suggested procedure for making texts workable and profitable for Intermediate Fluency students and native English speakers as well.

The teacher

- reviews the chapter and pulls out a manageable number of key concepts
- identifies vocabulary critical to talking and learning about the concepts
- assesses students' prior knowledge related to key concepts through student brainstorms, interest inventories, collaborative group discussions with realia serving as a visual trigger, and pair sharing (for example, "Tell your partner what you know about gold mining")
- gathers realia and visuals needed to make the text less abstract, getting them from students, a team teaching partner, a resource teacher, and parents
- leads a quick "text tour," focusing student attention on illustrations, chapter title and subtopics, bold-faced words, summary sections, and connection of chapter to theme, current events, previous chapters, activities, and concepts
- models mapping and note-taking techniques.

The students

- develop prediction questions in collaborative groups, pairs, or alone
- read a chapter on their own, with a language buddy, or listen to it via audiotape, recorded by classmate, cross-age tutor, or parent volunteer
- map the chapter
- answer prediction questions, generate and record additional questions, deposit words in a word bank, and make journal notes.

Throughout the chapter study, you'll want to kidwatch—watching, listening, and assessing what and how your students are learning. Listen to collaborative student groups find answers to their questions, look at their word bank deposits, read and answer their journal notes, and check and guide chapter mapping. By continuously looking at what students are saying and doing, you'll know when they have understood the key chapter concepts and are ready to move on.

Remember that the textbook is only one resource. Students experience the richness of language and learning when they're exposed to a variety of resources, including

- people
- CDs, cassettes
- films, slides, videotapes
- CD-ROMs
- online services
- encyclopedias, dictionaries
- closed-captioned TV
- dioramas
- photos
- collages, murals, sculptures
- masks, puppets
- paintings, drawings, etchings
- folktales, oral histories
- songs, instruments, concerts
- field trips, nature walks
- newspapers, magazines

- trade books, comics, cartoons
- histories, journals
- short stories, wordless books
- poems, letters
- still cameras, camcorders
- museums
- atlases, maps, globes
- costumes, props
- posters
- math manipulatives, calculators
- computers, printers
- phonebooks, cookbooks
- telescopes, microscopes
- construction tools
- e-mail, electronic pen-pals
- mysteries, biographies, autobiographies.

Field Notes: Teacher-To-Teacher

A field trip to the zoo, a wildlife video, an engaging story, or a collection of shells can become the source of a language experience story. Language experience stories use listening, speaking, reading, and writing in an integrated fashion. Students are involved in a shared experience and talk about their experiences and responses. The teacher guides group pre-writing activities and writes a group-dictated story with students. This story can be used as a reader, a source for vocabulary development, and a model for student writing. Motivation to read and re-read the story, to work with vocabulary from the story, and to study sentence structure is built-in, because the students are the authors of the story, and the experiences are their own.

Wendy Motoike
Encinita School
Rosemead, California

Develop key vocabulary. School success depends in large part on kids' ability to understand verbal and written explanations of concepts. One way to help second language learners with that understanding is to look at concepts in terms of key vocabulary. If we're teaching the concept of overpopulation, for example, we're likely to use terms such as *life span*, *environment*, *birth control*, *natural resources*, and *quality of life*. Students who are unclear on the key vocabulary would have little understanding of overpopulation. Here's one suggested route to develop key vocabulary with a tie-in to word banks:

1. Choose a manageable number of key vocabulary words for you and your students.

2. Make a list of objects and visuals you'll need to help explain the key vocabulary of an upcoming lesson. Get student volunteers to bring in as many of the items as possible.

3. Present key words when they occur within the context of the lesson or activity. Make the words as concrete as possible by hooking each to an object, model, photo, drawing, or movement.

4. Do a short lesson preview and review of the words only if you feel a presentation in the context of the regular lesson won't be enough to build meaning. Even with preview and review, maintain a meaningful activity context. Avoid drill.

5. Post the new key vocabulary in a prominent place in the classroom to create a collective word bank. A word bank is a spot where the entire class or individual students maintain groups of categorized, personally meaningful words connected to classroom and out-of-class activities; the class word bank adds to your print-rich environment. Collective word banks are often bubble-mapped, color-coded, and written in large, bold letters on pieces of butcher paper. The finished banks are taped to classroom walls.

6. Encourage students to select words they want to add to their personal word banks. How do they make word banks? Students can use an index card box, a section of a loose-leaf notebook, or a reserved spot in a journal. Have them connect a drawing or visual to words where needed. If they wish, students can briefly define the words with a synonym or a short blurb. Caution students against creating long lists of disconnected words with definitions copied from the dictionary. There are plenty of good student dictionaries available, including ones that have accompanying visuals with the traditional word definitions. These are especially helpful to second language students.

7. Encourage students to make "withdrawals" from their word banks whenever possible to make their discussion and writing more communicative. Interactive dialogue journals are a natural spot for students to use their key vocabulary for meaningful communication.

Online Resources

Still think a website is a home for a spider? If so, ask a teacher friend who's online to take you for a short spin on the information superhighway. The reaction of most first-time riders as they "surf the net" and explore the vast storehouse of education resources is an unrestrained "Wow!" In fact, I'm still wowed after four years of pulling items off the Internet to help me with my teaching.

Internet access cost is minimal, considering the benefits in information gained and the time saved in gaining it. For example, a third-fourth grade class in San José, California, made extensive use of the Internet this past year during a theme cycle on city planning. Students

- posted questions on architecture to a newsgroup (discussion forum)
- used English, Spanish, and Japanese to correspond with city planners in the U.S., Latin America, and Japan
- searched newspapers, the Smithsonian, and *National Geographic* for relevant articles
- examined current and historical city maps
- traded research findings and city design projects with another class across the country.

Besides enriching the curriculum and providing alternative ways for students to construct knowledge, accessing information online saved the teacher a considerable amount of time. She estimated that her two hours online saved her fifteen to twenty hours of preparation.

Online resources will also help you stay current on second language research and practice. You can download research abstracts and entire journal articles when you visit the applied linguistics resources on the World Wide Web (WWW), appropriately called Resources in Applied Linguistics (http://info-server.surrey.ac.uk/ELI/external.html). Click on the icon for Electronic Journals when you roll in. You'll find journals like *TESOL Journal* (Teachers of English to Speakers of Other Languages), *TESOL Quarterly*, and *TESL-EJ* (Teaching English as a Second Language—Electronic Journal). They all have easily searched indexes of current and past articles. A click on Archives at Resources in Applied Linguistics will lead you to a wealth of bilingual education resources. You can also access Educational Resources Information Center (ERIC) at this site. ERIC will e-mail you articles on every conceivable educational topic if requested. For more information on working with second language learners, click and zip on over to the Applied Linguistics WWW Virtual Library (http://alt.venus.co.uk/VL/AppLingBBK).

Go online to talk with other teachers who will help answer instructional questions you have. If you want to know how to use storytelling to help second-grade second language students with math word problems, post a question with a Usenet newsgroup. With this example, I'd try Teachers of ESL List (bit.listserv.tesl-l), Teaching English to Speakers of Other Languages (misc.education.language.english), and a community of storytellers (alt.arts.storytelling). I'd also try America Online, the nation's largest online service, to gather ideas from math teachers (route: Education...to Teacher's Network...to The Idea Exchange...to Mathematics). Wait a day or two after posting your question, then go back online. Chances are, a couple dozen responses will be waiting in your electronic mailbox. With all the newsgroups, you can search the list of posted topics and questions and perhaps find your question already answered.

Online services will also help your students connect to the local community and the world. One third-grade teacher I know arranges a monthly "virtual visitor" to dovetail with class activities. Past visitors have included the local town mayor, a city council member, a research biologist, a jazz musician, a children's book illustrator, and several authors. Students interact with the visitor online, posing questions and sharing the fruits of their investigations on target topics.

For teachers and students alike, online resources can also help with learning a second language. Want to improve your Arabic, Mandarin, Spanish, Ojibwa, or Vietnamese? Try the Human-Languages Page (http://www. june29. com/HLP/). You'll find spoken samples, software, magazines, newspapers, poetry, dictionaries, and tutorials on a whole host of languages—including Klingon from *Star Trek*! If you or your students would like to keyboard-talk in real time with speakers of another language, try one of the online language chat rooms. To visit with people in Japanese on America Online, for example, go to the International Channel...then International Bistro...then Japanese Chat. To find a Spanish-speaking "key-pal" on America Online for exchanges in non-real time (where you'll have all the time you want to write and figure out what's written back to you), go to International Channel...International Cafe...Español... Escribir... then Pen-Pal Exchange.

Here are some additional websites of particular interest to teachers working with second language learners.

- National Clearinghouse on Bilingual Education (NCBE) (http://www.ncbe.gwu.edu). Here you'll find anything and everything related to the exciting world of bilingual education and multilingualism. NCBE discussion groups include Early Bi-literacy, Educational Technology, Language Preservation, Special Education, and Refugee and Immigrant Education.

- National Center for Research on Cultural Diversity and Second Language Learning (http://zzyx.ucsc.edu/Cntr/cntr.html). This is a U.S. Department of Education center housed at the University of California, Santa Cruz. The site offers school project briefs from around the country, research reports, information on exemplary programs, practices, and teacher-training videos.

- *The Internet TESL Journal* (http://www.aitech.ac.jp/~iteslj/). Rather than a scholarly journal, this is a monthly magazine. It offers articles, lesson plans, class handouts, and plenty of project/activity ideas.

- Associations, Conferences, Journals, Newsgroups. This is a subpage of many TESL/TEFL/TESOL links (http://www.aitech.ac.jp/~iteslj/ESL3.html). Using information from this site, you could easily attend a conference per week year-round. Pack those bags!

- TESOL (http://www.ncbe.gwu.edu/tesol/). Visit this site and find selected journal articles, publications, and help with classroom applications.

- Dave's ESL Cafe (http://www.pacificnet.net/~sperling/links.html). Dave Sperling, an ESL instructor at California State University, Northridge, has created a site that manages to be as much fun as it is helpful. Walk in, grab a comfortable seat, and check out the idiom and joke pages, find lyrics to an old folksong, have your second language students trade stories with other second language learners, and spray paint your one-liners onto the ESL Graffiti Wall.

All the sites above provide links to numerous other topic-related sites. Explore and enjoy!

Making Small Groups More Effective

For second language students to successfully acquire English, they need to understand what you and other students say (comprehensible input), and they need to use language for real communication purposes (Krashen 1994).

One of the very best vehicles for that, of course, is small group work, especially collaborative learning activities where students have an authentic need to talk with one another, share materials and ideas, and pull together to problem solve and complete a given task.

Small group work, however, like any strategy we use, can go awry if we haven't laid the proper groundwork and attended to a few critical management issues. Here are some hints for ensuring successful small group work:

- Model all roles and tasks, including showing the end product.
- Model while seated at a table with kids grouped around you and when you're traveling around the room to check in with individual students and groups.
- Arrange the groups yourself sometimes. Other times, let students organize their own groups.
- Rotate roles and members of groups.
- Assign—or allow students to assign—tasks for each group member.
- Integrate bilingual or capable and sensitive monolingual buddies with second language learners.
- Discuss the group process with students—what worked and what didn't.
- Balance group work with large group, direct instruction, pair, and individual work.

It's understandable if you're a little skittish about increasing the amount of time your kids spend in small group work. If you have a number of second language learners, you might be concerned about how comprehensible group work is for them. Are they really "getting" the task and actively participating in the process? Moreover, new and veteran teachers alike experience periodic small group bomb-out with or without second language learners. If these bomb-outs are plentiful, teachers often abandon collaborative activities altogether, or at least drastically cut down on their frequency. Yet we all have a sense—that's backed up by solid research—that when collaborative groups work well, kids benefit tremendously with language, content, and social skill growth (Johnson, Johnson, Holubec and Roy 1984; Kagan 1986; Slavin 1991; Johns 1992).

A good way of ensuring successful group work is to talk to students about how to work with others, model appropriate behavior, and show them how to work collaboratively through role-playing.

We know that students working in successful groups

- ask questions
- discuss ideas with each other
- listen to each other
- share materials and information
- work together to solve problems
- demonstrate what they've learned.

D I A L O G U E

What do successful student groups do?

Yes   No

☐   ☐   Students share information and materials.

☐   ☐   Each student contributes to the product.

☐   ☐   Students know the language of facilitating, clarifying, and helping. They also understand what it means to gain consensus.

☐   ☐   Students use a wide range of print and nonprint resources.

☐   ☐   Students use a variety of ways to show what they've learned.

☐   ☐   Students discuss the group process—what worked and what didn't.

What am I doing to make collaborative groups successful? Do I model all the group roles? provide enough context clues? provide enough multilevel research material? allow sufficient time for questions and idea sharing? Do I lay out the task clearly?

_____

_____

_____

_____

Creating Planning Sheets for Learning Events

Here are two sample planning sheets for learning events from two different theme cycles. The first theme is animal behavior. Students choose what animals they wish to study. The second theme cycle is about solar energy. Place key concepts and skills at the top of the planning sheets. Many more concepts and skills unfold during the cycle, but these are the essential learnings we're shooting for—for all students.

Activities to answer kids' questions about the theme and to develop essential learnings are on the left side of the page. Context clues and materials needed to make those activities easy to understand and workable for second language learners (and probably most kids) are on the right.

In the real world of the classroom, I'd never type up all this information. I do use the planning sheet, or the back of a napkin, depending on where I'm doing the planning. Then I stick in the key concepts and skills and scratch in the context clues and materials I'm likely to forget without a written reminder.

Animal Behavior Planning Sheet: Crickets

Key Concepts and Skills

1. cricket anatomy, habits
2. observing and recording animal behavior
3. graphing, analyzing data
4. reporting out data
5. sense of story, story retelling
6. sharing/contrasting opinions

Activity	Context Clues and Materials
Cricket observation in student pairs (working like scientists)	• live crickets and food in jars (with lids!) • large cricket anatomy chart • What We Saw graph (overhead)
The Cricket's Pajamas by Deborah Hopkinson (storytelling)	• pajama sets (different sizes) • matchbook bed (with cotton) • small blue sheet • name tags and visuals (James, Mom Cricket) • sewing kit • story movements
The Cricket's Pajamas (big book)	• realia from above (with realia "pop-up" helpers)
Story review—Language Experience Approach (working like literary reviewers)	• kids perform and talk about their reactions to the story • story realia and visuals
Comparing—animal behavior in literature vs. the natural world	• story visuals • cricket behavior logs
Mindmapping for retelling (working like storytellers)	• colored pens for overhead • story realia and visuals • mindmap examples from other stories
Story retelling, collecting (working like storytellers)	• student mindmaps are guides for telling story to parents, siblings, friends

The K-2 cricket planning sheet provided about thirty minutes of activities each day for an entire week. The grades three-six solar energy sheet resulted in about one to two hours of activities per day for two weeks. Depending on grade and interest level, you and your kids may devote more or less time to these or similar units.

Energy Planning Sheet: Solar Energy

Key Concepts and Skills

1. sun as alternative energy source

2. nature of heat (radiation, conduction, convection)

3. lifestyle changes as a result of using solar energy

4. working/designing in small groups

5. construction techniques

6. hypothesizing, testing, data recording, analyzing

Activity	Context Clues and Materials
Solar Box Cooker (SBC) demonstrations	• SBC • baked apples!
Small group SBC construction Insulation experiments Temperature and time comparisons, graphing	• SBC construction examples and diagrams • cardboard, foil, glass, newspaper • variety of insulation materials • oven thermometer, stopwatch
Low-fat meal preparation in SBC SBC recipe doubling, tripling Taste-testing (foods cooked in SBC vs. regular oven)	• food items • recipe verb visuals (cut, sift, grate, add, stir, bake)
Guest expert from SBC International (geographical distribution of SBC project)	• SBC examples, slides
SBC impact reports on various habitats Oven/fuel survey through the ages/world regions	• maps, globe, habitat visuals • video clips and CD-ROM • reference books, *Smithsonian*, and and *National Geographic* articles
Student-prepared international feast for students and their families	• all SBC-cooked food!

Here's my rule of thumb on how much time to give a theme cycle: If kids are still fired up, still have questions they want answers to, I run longer with the theme. If interest is waning and the questions stop coming, we move on to something else. Like a lot of teachers, I gave up strict, predetermined activity timelines long ago. If we kidwatch carefully, students will let us know when a cycle change is really needed.

SHOPTALK

Bellanca, James. *The Cooperative Think Tank: Graphic Organizers to Teach Thinking in the Cooperative Classroom.* Palatine, Illinois: Skylight Publishing, 1990.

One of the enduring myths about beginning second language students is that they can't do critical thinking. Simple recall and labeling, yes, but forget any activities requiring analysis, synthesis, or evaluation. All students can and should do critical thinking. They can do a ton of it in their primary language, of course, and in English, too, if provided proper tools such as graphic organizers. Bellanca's book illustrates how teachers at all grade levels can use graphic organizers like the Ranking Ladder, Venn Diagrams, the Web, Pie Charts, and the Fish Bone to foster collaborative and sophisticated critical thinking across the curriculum. There is an important caveat, however: some of the organizers, such as the Right Angle or the Agree/Disagree Chart, require additional visuals—student and teacher drawings or magazine cut-outs, for example—to make them workable and effective for second language students. Bellanca includes several activity examples for each graphic tool presented. If only all teacher resource materials were this well-organized, readable, and helpful!

Chapter 5

Continuous Learning

Now that we've explored specific SLL instructional strategies, let's look at ways to support our students' learning process. Learning, after all, does not cease when the final bell rings at the end of the school day. Continuous learning requires continuous support—at school and at home.

Authentic Assessment

Authentic assessment—the rich documentation of student learning using multiple sources—is just as important for second language students as it is for their native English-speaking peers. The three big P's of authentic assessment—portfolios, projects, and performance-based testing—are especially effective in spotlighting the strengths of students just learning to speak their second language. A chronology of written and taped work, critiques of small group presentations and products, along with testing records showing the application of skills to real world problem solving give us tremendous insight into how well second language learners are doing with language and content acquisition. A lot more insight, many teachers would argue, than provided by formal language proficiency instruments or standardized, norm-referenced tests.

Let's look at alternatives to that traditional assessment mainstay, the narrative book report, as an example of how second language learners can expand the literacy spectrum and show us they understand the book's storyline, central conflict, character development, and key themes. Working alone, with a classmate, or in a small group, they might do one or more of the following:

- oral report with realia and visuals
- short role-play, longer scripted play, puppet play
- reader's theater, video and audio ("radio") productions
- slide or overhead projector reports
- character mindmaps, character interviews
- pantomime, dance
- storyboard, mural, diorama, sculpture, illustrations
- storyboard letter to author
- song, mini-opera
- chant, poem, rap.

With authentic assessment, both teacher and students are actively engaged in judging the quality and quantity of learning. Second language learners, just like other learners, do well with self, peer, and small group assessment if the yardstick for judging the value of student products is clearly understood, modeled by you or aides, and if second language students use their primary language when needed. Take a few moments to reflect on how you're currently assessing your second language learners. For more ideas on authentic assessment, see *Assessment: Continuous Learning* by Lois Bridges in

Field Notes: Teacher-To-Teacher

At the end of each unit we do an assessment activity where the students are asked to "show" what they have learned. They can make presentations using any art forms. We've had students create puppets, make books and poems, dance, use musical instruments, and create songs. We did our last study on immigrants. When we asked our students to show what they had learned, they used their different ways of knowing and created a drama of immigrants coming to America in a boat, wrote books, painted story pictures, drew portraits, and wrote songs and poetry. And these were just a few of their responses. What a sparkling time!

Joyce Caudill and Lisa Fulks
Kenwood Elementary School
Louisville, Kentucky

the Strategies for Teaching and Learning Professional Library; *What's Whole in Whole Language?* edited by Kenneth S. Goodman, Lois Bridges Bird, and Yetta M. Goodman; and *Authentic Assessment for English Language Learners: Practical Approaches for Teachers* by J. Michael O'Malley and Lorraine Valdez Pierce.

Six-year-old Tara, in Joyce Caudill and Lisa Fulks' class, shows she understands the concept of immigration as she uses writing and drawing to communicate in this good-bye note to her student teacher.

DIALOGUE

How do I gauge how well students are doing with curriculum concepts and skills? with second language growth?

_____

_____

How often do my second language students assess their own or their classmates' performance and products?

_____

_____

What questions do I have about assessing student portfolios, projects, and performance-based testing?

_____

_____

What additional support, such as planning time, workshops, demos, or coaching do I need to increase the breadth and depth of authentic assessment?

_____

_____

Giving Appropriate Homework

Because we're operating with one curriculum, it's best if we try to give the same homework assignments to all students, whenever possible. The assignments, however, like any of our in-class activities, must take into account students' widely differing English language proficiencies. That means we give a single homework assignment but offer kids some alternatives for it. Typical alternatives might include

- completing the assignment in the primary language, then bridging to the teacher through a bilingual classmate or an instructional aide
- writing via illustrations or illustrations plus some text
- reporting orally
- using the visual and performing arts to expand the literacy spectrum.

Regardless of the alternative used, the goal of the assignment remains the same for all students. Many traditional English print-bound assignments such as "Read Chapter 6 in your social studies book and answer the questions; do page 135 in the math book, word problems 1-8; and circle the answers on the Healthy Eating Worksheet," do not readily lend themselves to alternatives, especially when parallel material in the primary language is unavailable. But many more open-ended assignments that invite inquiry do. Here are some examples from K-6 classrooms. First I've listed assignments that kids do mostly alone, then you'll find some that produce and require a lot of family interaction. With only minor tinkering, many assignments can stretch over several grade levels. Students do the homework in the language they're most comfortable with.

Homework Examples: Student Working Mostly Alone

- Do some pleasure reading.
- Forecast the weather for a week, then check the paper each day to see how you did. Keep comparison records.
- Take your favorite comic strip from today's newspaper and make up new captions.
- Write out a justification for what you've told your parents you'd like to have—a new bike, an increase in allowance, new sneakers.
- Develop a personal weekly or monthly budget. Determine how much for treats, movie tickets, and the like.
- Write a thank-you letter to someone who recently did something nice for you; a fan letter to a favorite music, sports, or film star; a letter to the town mayor or city council about something that bugs you; a letter of complaint to some business that you think did not treat you fairly.
- Keep a secret or shared journal.
- Sort your small toys into bins and label them.
- Organize your collection (baseball cards, rocks, stamps). Inventory your collection and determine its current worth.
- Check the phone book to see if there are any clubs and organizations in the area offering activities related to your favorite hobby. Call or write for information.
- Make a graph of what you or the family pet eats for a week. Decide if the diet is a healthy one.
- For one week, keep a record of what television programs you watch. Categorize the programs (sitcoms, crime dramas, cartoons, nature shows) and figure out how much time you spend on each category. Decide if you need to change viewing habits or not.
- Search through a cookbook for new recipes to try. Create dinner menus for the week. Prepare a grocery list and estimate what the food will cost. Help shop and cook dinner!

- Estimate the number of minutes it will take you to do your household chores.
- Look up store numbers in the phone book and do some comparison shopping on an item you or your family wants to buy. Keep notes on the prices.
- With dates and captions, organize photos in a family album.

Homework Examples: Student Working with an Adult
- Read a favorite or new story together. Talk about what you've read.
- Discuss current events and compare your points of view.
- Take the major stories from the front page of the newspaper or lead stories on the evening news. On a globe or map, find where the stories originated.
- Talk about what happened at school and work. Trade questions and answers.
- Watch a favorite television show together. Pick a favorite character and explain your choice.
- Rate a movie or video on a scale of 1 to 10 and give specific reasons for your rating. Compare ratings with other family members and friends.
- Tell family history stories.
- Make up a song or ghost story together.
- Draw each other's portrait. Draw the family pet.
- Research and draw your family tree or family timeline including key events.
- Create a new recipe together, and record ingredients and amounts. Fix and rate the new dish.
- Document the typical day in the life of mom, dad, or other family member.

Again, whenever possible, homework for second language learners should be the same as for students who speak only English. Homework must be easy to understand, meaningful, and connected to the curriculum, targeting the same concepts and skills for all learners. In addition, the best SLL homework validates and builds on the students' home language and culture. Equally important, we'll want to design assignments that involve parents and family members. Support at home goes a long way toward supporting language and content development at school.

Getting most of your homework assignments to meet the above criteria can be tricky. If many assignments are falling short, the framework on page 107 may help. Once you've used the framework a couple times, you'll have the criteria down pat. Kiss the framework good-bye at that point. After all, in the real world of million-task teaching, who has the time to write all this stuff out anyway?

Homework Planning Framework

- Target Concept or Skill—What do we want kids to learn from the homework?
- Assignment—What will the kids actually do? on their own? with help? What will the end product be?
- Multiple Intelligences—What alternative learning tools (besides reading and writing) do we need to make the homework doable?
- Assessment—What will we assess? Who will conduct the assessment? the teacher? students? family members? peers?

Getting Family Members Involved

Here's the picture: you've got a class of thirty second graders, five primary languages, no aide, and a Paul Bunyan-size curriculum that just got bigger with last week's new health education mandate. You're on two school committees and one district task force. To top it off, you've just been tapped as the site union representative. That's when Mrs. Mendoza tells you she'd like to volunteer a couple of hours a day for the rest of the school year.

No doubt about it—you need help. In fact, without it, you're not sure if you'll survive till winter break. And you like including family members in the classroom. You encourage parents to visit and help out whenever they can. But since Mrs. Mendoza speaks very little English, you wonder how much help she'll be able to provide. Maybe she won't be much help at all. Maybe she won't understand how the typical American classroom operates. Maybe she'll add to your workload rather than reduce it. Maybe you should tell her thanks, but no thanks.

Concerns and worries like these are common. Getting past them can be tough, but worth it. If Mrs. Mendoza is brought into the system in a thoughtful, respectful way, if she's oriented to how school works, if guidelines and expectations are clear, and if her skills and strengths are valued and emphasized, chances are good that she'll be a valuable addition to the classroom. She'll provide help for kids, especially kids needing primary language support, and help for you as well.

Probably the best people to ask why parents are involved and how to increase that involvement are the involved parents themselves. A Central Valley school in California informally surveyed parents and found the following: A mom was able to volunteer only because the teacher was willing to let the mother bring her toddler along; a dad organized and led several activities for a fourth-grade class after hearing from the teacher that his hobbies—

metal detecting and pigeon breeding—could enliven the science and math curriculum; a bilingual mom regularly helped in the classroom and at home after the teacher explained how much her son and his Spanish-speaking class-mates needed her Spanish language expertise; a number of parents were able to attend night meetings once translation and child care were consistently provided. For more ideas on increasing parent involvement you might read David and Yvonne Freeman's book *Between Worlds: Access to Second Language Acquisition* and James Vopat's *The Parent Project: A Workshop Approach to Parent Involvement.*

S H O P T A L K

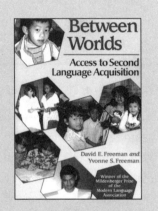

Freeman, David E. and Yvonne S. Freeman. *Between Worlds: Access to Second Language Acquisition.* Portsmouth, New Hampshire: Heinemann, 1995.

In exploring the "worlds" inside and outside the school, this book explains second language acquisition theory and examines various social and cultural factors that affect the academic performance of second language learners. The authors make theory come to life by focusing on second language learners who represent a range of ages, languages, and cultures. Using rich classroom examples, they illustrate how the social context of schooling influences academic outcomes. Not only do readers learn how to implement second language acquisition theory through effective instructional practices, they learn the critical importance of cultural sensitivity.

Hints for an Effective Family Volunteer Program
Do this:

- Ask an administrator or resource teacher to establish and maintain a volunteer program at the site, complete with training, reminder calls, and notes.
- Provide training on program elements, class rules, and how to help.
- Introduce the volunteer to students, give some background, explain what the person will be doing, and how lucky the class is to have the help of the volunteer.
- Give your volunteer an overview, goals, and directions for target activities.
- Let the volunteer really teach.

- Play to the volunteer's strengths—if he or she has a great science background, encourage the design of science activities.
- Encourage the volunteer—if bilingual—to use primary language skills.
- Give plenty of recognition—by telling family members how the volunteer is helping children learn, writing a note of thanks, arranging a special thank-you luncheon.

Avoid this:

- Overburdening the classroom teacher with the many tasks associated with a volunteer program.
- Letting the volunteer work in the classroom without training.
- Allowing a "mystery person" to suddenly float into the classroom and start helping.
- Letting the volunteer wing it.
- Always assigning secretarial tasks.
- Never letting the volunteer take initiative or offer ideas.
- Telling the volunteer to speak with students only in English.
- Taking the volunteer for granted.

Field Notes: Teacher-To-Teacher

I recently led a series of four Family Math workshops. In Family Math, adults and children come to school in the evenings and work collaboratively on manipulative-based math games and activities. All charts, graphs, and communication are provided in English, Spanish, and Vietnamese. Translators are provided at each session. As all participants felt valued, the series became low-risk, with a wonderful feeling of community. I especially enjoyed watching a group of Spanish-speaking women sort colored macaroni. They were having a wonderful time, talking nonstop. They understood what was going on and enjoyed practicing. With that kind of positive experience, they're far more likely to practice with their children—especially since I gave each family a bag of activity materials to take home.

Carol Wright
William Anderson Elementary
Lawndale, California

D I A L O G U E

What teacher, school, or district actions enable my students'
parents to become involved?

_____

_____

Is there a way to involve other parents using the same or similar
means?

_____

_____

What makes a parent get involved and stay involved?

_____

_____

Compare notes with your colleagues on parent involvement. What
has enabled parents to volunteer, come to meetings, and support
the SLL school program on the home front?

_____

_____

What has discouraged this involvement?

_____

_____

Empowerment for Second Language Learners

Educator and researcher Jim Cummins reminds us that human relationships lie at the heart of schooling. Negative, disrespectful interactions between teachers and students are disabling—both psychologically and
academically—and lead to school failure. Positive, respectful interactions
are empowering and lead to school success (Cummins 1994). For example, teachers who encourage primary language and culture, critical literacy, and parent involvement are more likely to have positive relationships
with their second language learners. Cummins cautions, however, that
empowerment isn't something that we should be doing "to" kids, as in

"Mr. Gustafson is going to empower Katrina this year." As we play the role of chief "empowerer" in the classroom, believing that empowerment must flow from teacher to student, we place students in a subordinate, passive position (Cummins 1996). What we're after is creating a community of learners where students are active agents of their own empowerment, where kids have the opportunities to personally construct the identity, knowledge, and skills necessary for their academic success. Approaches and strategies emphasized in this book, such as thematic instruction, the Natural Approach, process writing, and journal storyboarding can all serve as vehicles for active empowerment.

Empowerment for Second Language Learners	
Empowering Elements	**Disabling Elements**
• first language and home culture seen as strengths	• first language and home culture seen as a handicaps
• bilingual education, primary language support, and SDAIE	• sink-or-swim instruction
• additive bilingual education (maintenance)	• subtractive bilingual education (transitional)
• multicultural emphasis	• monocultural emphasis
• interactive and experiential methods that expand the literacy spectrum (collaborative learning, integrated thematic studies, process writing, multiple intelligences)	• transmission-mode "talk teaching"
• student experiences incorporated into curriculum	• student experiences excluded
• students help determine curriculum, learning goals	• students excluded from determining curriculum, learning goals
• family made active partners with school	• family excluded
• broad-based, authentic assessment	• overreliance on formal, paper and pencil testing

S H O P T A L K

Cummins, Jim. *Negotiating Identities: Education for Empowerment in a Diverse Society.* Los Angeles, California: California Association for Bilingual Education, 1996.

With *Negotiating Identities,* educator, theorist, and researcher Jim Cummins updates and expands his influential 1989 book, *Empowering Minority Students.* Finely crafted arguments, solid research, and real-world classroom examples help the author make a compelling case for his central contention, that academic success for culturally diverse students hinges, in large part, on the nature of power relations in the classroom. Coercive relations disempower students and increase the likelihood of failing in school. Collaborative relations empower and help students in school.

Establishing a classroom where collaborative power relations are the norm, where power is created and shared among students and teachers, is no easy matter. Teachers may have the motivation to go the collaborative direction, but not the means, especially if they're new to critical/transformative pedagogy. Cummins provides the means, offering a theoretical framework for collaborative empowerment and a wealth of ideas and strategies for implementing that framework in classrooms and schools.

This book shows ways of incorporating first language, strengthening the home-school connection, accelerating students' academic language learning, implementing a critical literacy model, and moving to non-discriminatory, advocacy-based assessment.

Especially helpful and inspiring are portraits of several preschool through secondary programs where teachers have created viable "contexts for collaborative empowerment"—classrooms where student identity is affirmed, critical inquiry is prized, and academic success in ensured.

"Case Studies" for Discussion

Read over each situation on the following pages. Though kids' names and some details have been changed, the situations are real, sometimes a little too real. Decide if the situation empowers or disables second language learners. What is the teacher and school specifically doing to help ensure academic success or make it less likely? For disabling situations, what suggestions could you give the teacher and school to turn the situation around to open the academic door—and keep it open—for second language learners?

1. María seems to understand the directions to assignments, but rarely, if ever, turns in completed work. Her fifth-grade teacher assigns one of her bilingual classmates, a "language buddy," to help María in class.

2. A volunteer aide helps the teacher for a couple hours each day. The aide is fully bilingual but is reluctant to use her Vietnamese because she doesn't want Vietnamese to become a "crutch" for any of the students. The K-1 teacher is thankful for any help he can get, so despite what he knows about the importance of primary language support, he lets the aide work with students wholly in English.

3. Ten-year-old Shigeo is brand-new to the country and to English. One day after enrollment, he is run through a large battery of tests in English: oral proficiency, reading comprehension, writing, and math. The test administrator sees the boy's shaken, sorrowful look at the end of the session. Communicating through a bilingual aunt who's brought Shigeo to school that day, the tester tells him he did really great on everything.

4. Every so often the fifth-grade teacher tries to get a point across to her Latino second language learners in broken Spanish. The students catch only about ten percent of her Spanish.

5. Sixth-grader Griselda won't speak in class—in English or Spanish. She's failing nearly every class. She's told two teachers that she doesn't care about learning English at all. She seems uninterested in all subjects, even those that are heavily sheltered. Her literature teacher reports that Griselda was "pretty enthused" with a story she wrote about a local gang incident. The teacher is worried, however, that Griselda will never want to write about anything other than gangs if she encourages her in that direction. The teacher tells her she can do one more gang topic story, but only one.

6. The teacher always asks one of her students, Kei, to translate key points for her Cantonese speaking second graders.

7. Because Tomás and Kou don't have English literacy skills, the teacher suggests they take a pantomime part in their group's play production.

8. The fifth-sixth grade combination teacher has high expectations for all students, including second language learners. He expects students to listen to the directions carefully, ask questions if they're lost, and produce the required work. Two recently arrived second

language learners are not living up to his expectations. They've begun to act out in class and have started teasing other students who are trying their best to learn. After several futile heart-to-heart talks with the students and calls home that produce no change in behavior, the teacher considers the two students "guaranteed dropouts."

9. The teacher lets first-grader Hee Sun share a long story about a family incident in his home country even though the story only marginally relates to the lesson at hand.

10. Three or four times a week, the kindergarten-first grade teacher has her second language students teach their monolingual peers a song, poem, or some key vocabulary terms in Spanish, Mandarin, or Tagalog.

11. The teacher has learned that Bao, a newly arrived Laotian student, is really interested in science, but won't ask him anything during science activities because she's worried she might embarrass him somehow. The teacher is waiting until Bao "has a lot more English and feels comfortable with things."

12. The teacher encourages Maricela to report the results of her group's research in Spanish, while an accompanying English translation is provided by a bilingual student.

13. Two highly disaffected fifth-grade second language learners were caught "tagging" the back wall of the multi-purpose room. The principal subsequently asks them to help him translate school notices every so often. He also asks them to consider doing a couple

S H O P T A L K

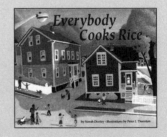

Dooley, Norah. *Everybody Cooks Rice.* Minneapolis, Minnesota: Carolrhoda Books, 1991.

It's time for dinner, and Carrie's mom sends her out to find her wayward younger brother. As Carrie goes from house to house in the multiethnic neighborhood, she finds each family cooking a different but tasty rice dish. This book is great for helping all children appreciate the differences and similarities among groups in our increasingly multicultural society. By the end of the book, you and the kids will be plenty hungry. No problem—the author includes simple-to-follow recipes for each delicious dish. Happy reading and happy eating!

bilingual guest shot articles for the school newspaper on topics that the regular reporters typically do not cover.

14. Pablo and Blas speak a lot of Spanish in class. Their third-grade teacher wants them to use more English and periodically reminds them that "you've got to speak English in school if you really want to learn."

15. The second-grade teacher notices that Beatriz, the new student from Cuba, is gifted in the visual arts but has yet to speak any English. The teacher encourages Beatriz to use and share her talents with classmates and assigns Beatriz a language buddy.

Closing Reflections

Nearly twenty-five years ago, straight out of college and with the ink still wet on my credential, I convinced a school district to take a chance on me. I was ready to teach! After all, I'd been through a university teacher preparation program, completed my student teaching, and read a wagon-load of how-to-teach books.

I entered the classroom, armed with tons of strategies, techniques, and teaching tips. Like many new and inexperienced teachers, I was ready to set the world on fire. The inevitable upshot, of course, is that I created lots of smoke and few flames. My book understanding of theory-informed instruction rarely translated into quick success with my students. It took time to learn the ins and outs and dos and don'ts of every instructional strategy I gallantly tried to implement. It took time to get things right. And it still does. Fast-forwarding a quarter century to the present, I find that I still need lots of trial-and-error time with new instructional ideas and strategies before I can comfortably use them to make a difference for students.

As you consider what you'd like to take from this book, give yourself the gift of time to implement new strategies and techniques. If you're new to teaching or to any of the ideas in the book, you'll need lots of classroom try-out time before the strategies and techniques become an effective part of your instructional repertoire. We all know what it's like to read something in a book, try it out in our own classrooms, and experience less than successful teaching. And sometimes new ideas don't work well the second or even the third time we try them. But as you keep plugging away, striving to revise and refine both your professional understandings and practice, you'll discover that things get easier.

In addition to reading professional literature, effective teachers spend time carefully observing their students, sharing and discussing critical practices with their colleagues, and engaging in thoughtful self-evaluation and revision.

As you adapt the strategies in this book and make them your own in ways that support you and your students' unique needs and interests, you'll discover brand new ways of bringing second language learners into the core curriculum. I wish you much success as you work with all your students—those who are learning a second language, and native English speakers too!

Professional Development Needs Self-Inventory

- Consider the knowledge, skills, strategies, and techniques you have now for meeting the needs of second language learners.
- Think about what you still want to learn and about the support and resources you'll need to increase effectiveness.
- For each area listed below, note your degree of need. Share the results with your peer coach and administrator.

Need Area	Degree of Need			
	High	Medium	Low	No Need
program planning, program models	☐	☐	☐	☐
informal and formal language assessment	☐	☐	☐	☐
interactive strategies and techniques	☐	☐	☐	☐
second language acquisition theory	☐	☐	☐	☐
oral and literacy development across the curriculum	☐	☐	☐	☐
thematic instruction	☐	☐	☐	☐
development of children's multiple intelligences	☐	☐	☐	☐
class management, lesson design	☐	☐	☐	☐
authentic assessment	☐	☐	☐	☐
materials survey and evaluation	☐	☐	☐	☐
establishing a peer-coaching team and release time	☐	☐	☐	☐
consultative coaching (observation and feedback)	☐	☐	☐	☐
demo teaching (with your students)	☐	☐	☐	☐
multicultural information on target groups	☐	☐	☐	☐
other _____				

Professional Bibliography

Armstrong, Thomas. *Multiple Intelligences in the Classroom*. Alexandria, Virginia: Association for Supervision and Curriculum Development, 1994.

Asher, James. *Learning Another Language through Actions: The Complete Teacher's Guidebook*. Los Gatos, California: Sky Oaks Productions, 1977.

————. "The Total Physical Response Approach," *Innovative Approaches to Language Teaching*, edited by Robert W. Blair. Rowley, Massachusetts: Newbury House, 1982.

————. "The Total Physical Response Approach to Second Language Learning," *Modern Language Journal 53*, Issue 1 1969.

Atwell, Nancie. *Side by Side: Essays on Teaching To Learn*. Portsmouth, New Hampshire: Heinemann, 1991.

Baker, Colin. *Foundations of Bilingual Education and Bilingualism*. Clevedon, Avon, England: Multilingual Matters, 1993.

Bellanca, James. *The Cooperative Think Tank: Graphic Organizers To Teach Thinking in the Cooperative Classroom*. Palatine, Illinois: Skylight Publishing, 1990.

Bridges, Lois. *Assessment: Continuous Learning*. Strategies for Teaching and Learning Professional Library, The Galef Institute. York, Maine: Stenhouse Publishers, 1995.

———. *Creating Your Classroom Community*. Strategies for Teaching and Learning Professional Library, The Galef Institute. York, Maine: Stenhouse Publishers, 1995.

———. *Writing as a Way of Knowing*. Strategies for Teaching and Learning Professional Library, The Galef Institute. York, Maine: Stenhouse Publishers, 1997.

Bridges Bird, Lois, ed. *Becoming a Whole Language School: The Fair Oaks Story*. Katonah, New York: Richard C. Owen, 1989.

Brown, H. Douglas. *Principles of Language Learning and Teaching*. 3d ed. Englewood Cliffs, New Jersey: Prentice Hall, 1994.

Brown, Roger. *A First Language: The Early Stages*. Cambridge, Massachusetts: Harvard University Press, 1973.

Brumfit, Christopher. "Review of Stephen Krashen's Language Acquisition and Language Education," *Applied Linguistics 13*, March 1992.

Burnham, Laurene and Muriel Peña. "Effects of Bilingual Instruction on English Academic Achievement of LEP Students." Baldwin Park, California: Baldwin Park Unified School District, 1986.

Caine, Renate Nummela and Geoffrey Caine. *Education on the Edge of Possibility*. Alexandria, Virginia: Association for Supervision and Curriculum Development, 1997.

California Department of Education. *Bilingual Education Handbook: Designing Instruction for LEP Students*. Sacramento: California Department of Education, 1990.

California Department of Education. *Language Census Report for California Public Schools*. Sacramento: California Department of Education, 1996.

Celce-Murcia, Marianne, ed. *Teaching English as a Second or Foreign Language*. 2d ed. Boston, Massachusetts: Heinle and Heinle, 1991.

Collier, Virginia. "A Synthesis of Studies Examining Long-term Language-Minority Student Data on Academic Achievement," *Bilingual Research Journal 16*, Winter-Spring 1992.

Crawford, James. *Bilingual Education: History, Politics, Theory, and Practice*. 3d ed. Los Angeles, California: Bilingual Educational Services, 1995.

Cummins, Jim. *Bilingual and Minority-Language Children*. Toronto: OISE Press, 1981.

———. "The Cross-lingual Dimensions of Language Proficiency: Implications for Bilingual Education and the Optimal Age Issue," *TESOL Quarterly 14*, June 1980.

———. *Empowering Minority Students*. Sacramento: California Association for Bilingual Education, 1989.

————. *Negotiating Identities: Education for Empowerment in a Diverse Society*. Ontario, California: California Association for Bilingual Education, 1996.

————. "The Role of Primary Language Development in Promoting Educational Success for Language Minority Students," *Schooling and Language Minority Students: A Theoretical Framework*. 2d ed. Office of Bilingual Bicultural Education. Los Angeles: Evaluation, Dissemination and Assessment Center, California State University, 1994.

Daly, Elizabeth, ed. *Monitoring Children's Language Development: Holistic Assessment in the Classroom*. Portsmouth, New Hampshire: Heinemann, 1989.

Delgado-Gaitan, Concha. *Literacy for Empowerment: The Role of Parents in Children's Education*. New York: The Falmer Press, 1990.

Edelsky, Carole. *Writing in a Bilingual Program: Había Una Vez*. Norwood, New Jersey: Ablex, 1986.

Edelsky, Carole, Sarah Hudelson, Barbara Flores, Florence Barkin, Bess Altwerger and Kristina Jilbert. "Semilingualism and Language Deficit," *Applied Linguistics 4*, Spring 1983.

Edelsky, Carole, Bess Altwerger and Barbara Flores. *Whole Language: What's the Difference?* Portsmouth, New Hampshire: Heinemann, 1991.

Edwards, Betty. *Drawing on the Right Side of the Brain*. Los Angeles: Tarcher, 1989.

Egan, Kieran. *Teaching as Storytelling: An Alternative Approach to Teaching and Curriculum in the Elementary School*. Chicago: The University of Chicago Press, 1986.

Emberley, Ed. *Ed Emberley's Drawing Book of Animals*. New York: Scholastic, 1970.

Flemming, Donald, Lucie Germer and Christiane Kelley. *All Things to All People: A Primer for K-12 ESL Teachers in Small Programs*. Alexandria, Virginia: TESOL, 1993.

Frederickson, Jean, ed. *Reclaiming Our Voices: Bilingual Education, Critical Pedagogy and Praxis*. Ontario, California: California Association for Bilingual Education, 1995.

Frederickson, Nora and Tony Cline. *Curriculum Related Assessment with Bilingual Children*. London: University College, 1990.

Freeman, David E. and Yvonne S. Freeman. *Between Worlds: Access to Second Language Acquisition*. Portsmouth, New Hampshire: Heinemann, 1994.

————. *Whole Language for Second Language Learners*. Portsmouth, New Hampshire: Heinemann, 1992.

Freire, Paulo. *Pedagogy of the Oppressed*. New York: Seabury, 1970.

Gardner, Howard. *Frames of Mind: The Theory of Multiple Intelligences*. New York: Basic Books, 1983.

———. *Frames of Mind: The Theory of Multiple Intelligences*. With a new introduction by the author. New York: Basic Books, 1993.

Gibbons, Pauline. *Learning To Learn in a Second Language*. Portsmouth, New Hampshire: Heinemann, 1993.

Goodman, Kenneth S. *What's Whole in Whole Language?* Portsmouth, New Hampshire: Heinemann, 1986.

Goodman, Kenneth S., Lois Bridges Bird and Yetta M. Goodman, eds. *The Whole Language Catalog*. New York: Macmillan-McGraw Hill, 1991.

———. *The Whole Language Catalog: Supplement on Authentic Assessment*. New York: Macmillan-McGraw Hill, 1992.

Goodman, Kenneth S., Yetta M. Goodman and Barbara Flores. *Reading in the Bilingual Classroom*. Rosslyn, Virginia: National Clearinghouse for Bilingual Education, 1979.

Graves, Donald. *Writing: Children and Teachers at Work*. Portsmouth, New Hampshire: Heinemann, 1983.

Hakuta, Kenji. *Mirror of Language: The Debate on Bilingualism*. New York: Basic Books, 1986.

Hamilton, Mary, David Barton and Roz Ivanic, eds. *Worlds of Literacy*. Clevedon, Avon, England: Multilingual Matters, 1994.

Hart, Leslie. *Human Brain and Human Learning*. Village of Oak Creek, Arizona: Books for Educators, 1983.

Heller, Paul G. *Drama as a Way of Knowing*. Strategies for Teaching and Learning Professional Library, The Galef Institute. York, Maine: Stenhouse Publishers, 1995.

Herbert, Charles. *Final Evaluation Report: Bilingual Basic Grant Project, ESEA Title VII*. San Diego, California: San Diego Schools, 1986.

Holt, Daniel, ed. *Cooperative Learning: A Response to Linguistic and Cultural Diversity*. Washington, D.C.: Center for Applied Linguistics, 1993.

Hudelson, Sarah. "Kan Yu Ret an Rayt en Ingles: Children Become Literate in English as a Second Language." *TESOL Quarterly 18*, June 1984.

Johns, Kenneth. "Mainstreaming Language Minority Students through Cooperative Grouping," *The Journal of Educational Issues of Language Minority Students 11*, July 1992.

Johnson, David, Roger Johnson, Edythe Johnson Holubec and Patricia Roy. *Circles of Learning: Cooperation in the Classroom*. Alexandria, Virginia: Association for Supervision and Curriculum Development, 1984.

Johnson, Terry D. and Daphne R. Louis. *Literacy through Literature*. Portsmouth, New Hampshire: Heinemann, 1987.

Kagan, Spencer. "Cooperative Learning and Sociocultural Factors in Schooling," *Beyond Language: Social and Cultural Factors in Schooling Language Minority Students*. Los Angeles: Evaluation, Dissemination and Assessment Center, California State University, 1986.

King, Edith, Marilyn Chipman and Marta Cruz-Janzen. *Educating Young Children in a Diverse Society*. Boston: Allyn and Bacon, 1994.

Krashen, Stephen. *Inquiries and Insights*. Hayward, California: Alemany Press, 1985.

——. "Bilingual Education and Second Language Acquisition Theory," *Schooling and Language Minority Students: A Theoretical Framework*. 2d ed. Los Angeles: Evaluation, Dissemination and Assessment Center, California State University, 1994.

——. *The Power of Reading*. Englewood, Colorado: Libraries Unlimited, 1993.

——. *Principles and Practice in Second Language Acquisition*. New York: Pergamon Press, 1982.

Krashen, Stephen and Douglas Biber. *On Course: Bilingual Education's Success in California*. Sacramento: California Association for Bilingual Education, 1988.

Krashen, Stephen and Tracy Terrell. *The Natural Approach: Language Acquisition in the Classroom*. Englewood Cliffs, New Jersey: Alemany Press, 1983.

Legarreta, Dorothy. "The Effects of Program Models on Language Acquisition by Spanish-Speaking Children," *TESOL Quarterly 13*, December 1979.

Lessow-Hurley, Judith. *The Foundations of Dual Language Instruction*. New York: Longman, 1990.

Leyba, Charles F. *Longitudinal Study, Title VII Bilingual Program*. Santa Fe Public Schools, Santa Fe, New Mexico. Los Angeles: National Dissemination and Assessment Center, California State University, 1978.

Leyba, Charles F., ed. *Schooling and Language Minority Students: A Theoretical Framework*. 2d ed. Los Angeles: Evaluation, Dissemination and Assessment Center, California State University, 1994.

Littlewood, William. *Communicative Language Teaching: An Introduction*. Cambridge: Cambridge University Press, 1991.

Lonergan, Jack. *Video in Language Teaching*. Cambridge: Cambridge University Press, 1993.

Marks-Tarlow, Terry. *Creativity Inside Out: Learning through Multiple Intelligences*. New York: Innovative Learning Publications, 1996.

McLaughlin, Barry. "Conscious Versus 'Unconscious' Learning," *TESOL Quarterly 24*, Winter 1990.

National Standards in Foreign Language Education Project. *Standards for Foreign Language Learning: Preparing for the 21st Century*. Yonkers, New York: National Standards in Foreign Language Education Project, 1996.

Office of Bilingual Bicultural Education. *Schooling and Language Minority Students: A Theoretical Framework*. 1st ed. Los Angeles: Evaluation, Dissemination and Assessment Center, California State University, Los Angeles, 1981.

Ohanian, Susan. *Math as a Way of Knowing*. Strategies for Teaching and Learning Professional Library, The Galef Institute. York, Maine: Stenhouse Publishers, 1995.

Oller, John and Patricia Richard-Amato, eds. *Methods That Work: Ideas for Literacy and Language Teachers*. Boston: Heinle and Heinle, 1993.

O'Malley, J. Michael and Lorraine Valdez Pierce. *Authentic Assessment for English Language Learners: Practical Approaches for Teachers*. Reading, Massachusetts: Addison-Wesley, 1996.

Page, Nick. *Music as a Way of Knowing*. Strategies for Teaching and Learning Professional Library, The Galef Institute. York, Maine: Stenhouse Publishers, 1995.

Peyton, Joy and Leslee Reed. *Dialogue Journal Writing with Non-native English Speakers: A Handbook for Teachers*. Alexandria, Virginia: TESOL, 1990.

Pinker, Steven. *The Language Instinct: How the Mind Creates Language*. New York: William Morrow, 1994.

———. *Language Learnability and Language Development*. Cambridge, Massachusetts: Harvard University Press, 1984.

Ramírez, J. David. "Final Report: Longitudinal Study of Structured English Immersion Strategy, Early-Exit and Late-Exit Bilingual Education Programs." Washington, D.C.: U.S. Department of Education, 1991.

Rivers, Wilga. *Interactive Language Teaching*. Cambridge: Cambridge University Press, 1992.

Samway, Katharine Davies and Gail Whang. *Literature Study Circles in a Multicultural Classroom*. York, Maine: Stenhouse Publishers, 1996.

Saville-Troike, Muriel. "What Really Matters in Second Language Learning for Academic Achievement?" *TESOL Quarterly 18*, June 1984.

Schifini, Alfredo. *Sheltered English: Content Area Instruction for Limited English Proficient Students*. Downey, California: Los Angeles County Office of Education, 1988.

Seely, Contee and Elizabeth Romijn. *TPR Is More than Commands—at All Levels*. Berkeley, California: Command Performance Language Institute, 1995.

Short, Kathy G. *Literature as a Way of Knowing*. Strategies for Teaching and Learning Professional Library, The Galef Institute. York, Maine: Stenhouse Publishers, 1997.

Skutnabb-Kangas, Tove and Pertti Toukomaa. *Teaching Migrant Children's Mother Tongue and Learning the Language of the Host Country in the Context of the Sociocultural Situation of the Migrant Family*. Helsinki: The Finnish National Commission for UNESCO, 1976.

Slavin, Robert E. "A Synthesis of Research on Cooperative Learning," *Educational Leadership* 48, February 1991.

Smith, Frank. *Insult to Intelligence: The Bureaucratic Invasion of Our Classrooms*. Portsmouth, New Hampshire: Heinemann, 1986.

———. *Reading without Nonsense*. New York: Teachers College Press, 1985.

Snow, Catherine E., Herlinda Cancino, Jeanne De Temple and Sara Schley. "Giving Formal Definitions: A Linguistic or Metalinguistic Skill?," *Language Processing in Bilingual Children*, edited by Ellen Bialystok. Cambridge: Cambridge University Press, 1991.

Stempleski, Susan and Paul Arcario, eds. *Video in Second Language Teaching: Using, Selecting, and Producing Video for the Classroom*. Alexandria, Virginia: TESOL, 1992.

Stenmark, Jean, Virginia Thompson and Ruth Cossey. *Family Math*. Berkeley, California: Lawrence Hall of Science, University of California, Berkeley, 1986.

Sylvester, Robert. *A Celebration of Neurons: An Educator's Guide to The Human Brain*. Alexandria, Virginia: Association for Supervision and Curriculum Development, 1995.

Terrell, Tracy. "The Natural Appoach in Bilingual Education," *Schooling and Language Minority Students: A Theoretical Framework*. 1st ed. Los Angeles: Evaluation, Dissemination and Assessment Center, California State University, 1981.

Terrell, Tracy. "A Natural Approach to Second Language Acquisition and Learning," *Modern Language Journal* 41, November 1977.

TESOL Publications. *ESL Standards for Pre-K–12 Students*. Alexandria, Virginia: TESOL.

Thomas, Wayne P. and Virginia P. Collier. "Research Summary of Study in Progress: Language Minority Student Achievement and Program Effectiveness." Summary of presentation at the California Association of Bilingual Education, Anaheim, California: 1995.

Tollefson, James. *Planning Language, Planning Inequality: Language Policy in the Community*. New York: Longman, 1991.

Vopat, James. *The Parent Project: A Workshop Approach to Parent Involvement*. York, Maine: Stenhouse Publishers, 1994.

Williams, Linda. *Teaching for the Two-sided Mind: A Guide to Right Brain/Left Brain Education*. New York: Simon and Schuster, 1983.

Wortman, Robert. *Administrators: Supporting School Change*. Strategies for Teaching and Learning Professional Library, The Galef Institute. York, Maine: Stenhouse Publishers, 1995.

Zakkai, Jennifer Donohue. *Dance as a Way of Knowing*. Strategies for Teaching and Learning Professional Library, The Galef Institute. York, Maine: Stenhouse Publishers, 1997.

Children's Bibliography

Ada, Alma Flor. *My Name Is María Isabel*. Illustrated by Kathryn Dyble Thompson. New York: Aladdin, 1995. Third grader María Isabel, who was born in Puerto Rico and now lives in the United States, wants the teacher to call her by her real name. The writing assignment "My Favorite Wish" helps her show the teacher how much of our self-identity comes wrapped in a name.

Altman, Linda Jacobs. *Amelia's Road*. Illustrated by Enrique O. Sanchez. New York: Lee and Low Books, 1993. Tired of moving around so much, Amelia, the daughter of migrant farm workers, dreams of a stable home.

Anno, Masaichiro and Mitsumasa. *Anno's Mysterious Multiplying Jar*. Illustrated by Mitsumasa Anno. New York: Philomel, 1983. Simple text and pictures introduce the mathematic concept of factorials.

Anonymous. *Celebrando el Año Nuevo: La Señorita Yuan-Shiau* (Celebrating New Year: Miss Yuan-Shiau). Cerritos, California: Wonder Kids, 1992. Written in both English and Spanish, these two tales each tell a story about the Chinese New Year.

Anonymous. *El Hermano Gato y el Hermano Ratón: Las Astas Del Gallo* (Brother Cat and Brother Rat: The Rooster's Antlers). Cerritos, California: Wonder Kids, 1992. These two Chinese legends, written in both Spanish and English, teach childen the importance of keeping their word.

Blanco, Alberto. *La Sirena del Desierto* (The Desert Mermaid). Illustrated by Patricia Revah. San Francisco: Children's Book Press, 1992. A desert mermaid living in an oasis seeks to save her people by rediscovering the forgotten songs of their ancestors.

Brown, Richard. *100 Words about Working*. San Diego: Harcourt Brace Jovanovich, 1988. Labeled illustrations depict people performing their various jobs. Children gain a sense of the vast number of jobs in the world.

Bunting, Eve. *How Many Days to America?* Illustrated by Beth Peck. New York: Clarion Books, 1988. This book tells of a family fleeing their native homeland to find political refuge in America. It is a simple story that can help children explore the important issue of immigration as it applies to all people.

Carle, Eric. *The Very Hungry Caterpillar*. New York: Philomel, 1969. Follow the progress of a hungry caterpillar as he eats his way through a varied and large quantity of food.

Cleary, Beverly. *Ramona and Her Father*. Illustrated by Alan Tiegreen. New York: Morrow Junior, 1977. When Ramona's father unexpectedly loses his job, the family routine is upset during Ramona's second-grade year.

Cohen, Barbara. *Molly's Pilgrim*. Illustrated by Michael J. Deraney. New York: William Morrow, 1983. An American third-grade class learns the true meaning of Thanksgiving with the help of Molly, a recent immigrant from Russia.

Collington, Peter. *The Angel and the Soldier Boy*. New York: Dragonfly, 1987. A child dreams her toy angel and soldier come alive in a perilous adventure in which they rescue a coin from thieving pirates.

Delacre, Lulu. *Vejigantes Masquerade*. New York: Scholastic, 1992. This bilingual tale from Puerto Rico tells the story of a very clever boy who manages to make his own costume for the carnival. Children learn what a *vejigante* is and how to make their own festive mask.

Dooley, Norah. *Everybody Cooks Rice*. Illustrated by Peter J. Thornton. Minneapolis, Minnesota: Carolrhoda Books, 1991. A child is sent to find her younger brother at dinnertime and discovers that although each family in her neighborhood is from a different country, everyone is preparing rice. The book concludes with a variety of rice recipes.

Dorros, Arthur. *Abuela*. Illustrated by Elisa Kleven. New York: Dutton Children's, 1991. While riding on a bus with her grandmother, a little girl imagines that they are carried up into the sky and fly over New York City.

Ekoomiak, Normee. *Arctic Memories*. New York: Henry Holt, 1988. Text in both Inuktitut and English describes a now vanished way of life for the Inuit. Remarkable art, including drawings, paintings, and embroidered and appliquéd wall hangings, complement the text.

García, Richard. *My Aunt Otilia's Spirits*. Illustrated by Robin Cherin and Roger I. Reyes. San Francisco: Children's Book Press, 1987. The wall knockings and bed shakings that always accompany Aunt Otilia's visits do not bother a young boy until the night he sees her skeleton leave her body.

Garza, Carmen Lomas. *Family Pictures: Cuadros de Familia*. San Francisco: Children's Book Press, 1990. With vivid illustrations and bilingual text, the author describes her experiences growing up in a Latino community in Texas.

George, Jean Craighead. *Julie of the Wolves*. Illustrated by John Schoenherr. New York: Harper and Row, 1972. While running away from home and an unwanted marriage, a thirteen-year-old Eskimo girl becomes lost on the North slope of Alaska and is befriended by a wolf pack.

Greenfield, Eloise. *Africa Dream*. Illustrated by Carole Byard. New York: The John Day Company, 1977. An African American child's dreams are filled with the images of the people and places of Africa.

Hammond, Anna and Joe Matunis. *Esta Casa Que Hemos Hecho* (This Home We Have Made). New York: Crown, 1993. Inspired by a mural in New York City painted largely by formerly homeless children, this is the story of a homeless child who joins a magical parade in hopes of finding a home of her own. A testament to the inspirational role art can play in the lives of children.

Harvey, Diane Kelsay and Bob Harvey. *El Misterio de Melodía* (Melody's Mystery). Wilsonville, Oregon: Beautiful America, 1991. In English and Spanish text, this book presents the life cycle of a monarch butterfly, with magnificent full-color photographs.

Hoban, Tana. *I Read Symbols*. New York: Greenwillow Books, 1983. Tana Hoban's photographs stimulate discussion about the meanings of international signs and symbols that are a part of children's everyday lives.

Hopkinson, Deborah. *The Cricket's Pajamas*. Illustrated by David McPhail. Ladybug Magazine, Pern, Illinois: Carus, 1990. A little boy and a cricket help each other fall asleep in this tender and affecting short story.

Keats, Jack Ezra. *Over in the Meadow*. New York: Four Winds Press, 1971. A book of verses that describe the activities of various animals.

Kuklin, Susan. *How My Family Lives in America*. New York: Bradbury Press, 1992. African American, Asian American, and Latino American children describe their families' cultural traditions.

Lee, Jeanne. *Toad Is the Uncle of Heaven*. New York: Henry Holt, 1985. Toad leads a group of animals to ask the King of Heaven to send rain to the parched earth. A Vietnamese folktale.

Lord, Bette Bao. *In the Year of the Boar and Jackie Robinson*. Illustrated by Marc Simont. New York: Harper and Row, 1984. In 1947, a Chinese child comes to Brooklyn, where she learns about American culture—at school, in her apartment building, and through her love for baseball.

Maxner, Joyce. *Nicholas Cricket*. Illustrated by William Joyce. New York: HarperCollins, 1983. Nicholas Cricket and the other members of the Bug-a-Wug Cricket Band lead all the forest creatures in a musical celebration of the night.

McDermott, Gerald. *Flecha al Sol* (Arrow to the Sun). New York: Viking, 1991. An adaption of the Pueblo Indian myth which explains how the spirit of the Lord of the Sun was brought to the living world.

Mendez, Phil. *The Black Snowman*. Illustrated by Carole Byard. New York: Scholastic, 1989. Through the powers of a magical kente, a black snowman comes to life and helps young Jacob discover the beauty of his African American heritage as well as his own self-worth.

Mohr, Nicholasa. *Felita*. Illustrated by Ray Cruz. New York: Dial Press, 1979. A delightful story about the everyday experiences of an eight-year-old Puerto Rican girl growing up in a close-knit, urban community.

Morris, Ann. *Hats, Hats, Hats*. Photographs by Ken Heyman. New York: Lothrop, Lee and Shepard, 1989. Ken Heyman's photographs show the many different hats worn around the world and the reasons for wearing them. An illustrated index provides location and cultural information.

Pomerantz, Charlotte. *The Tamarindo Puppy and Other Poems*. Illustrated by Byron Barton. New York: Greenwillow Books, 1980. With natural humor and lively rhythm, these thirteen joyous poems move effortlessly from English to Spanish and back again, much the way many bilingual people do.

Reiser Lynn. *Margarita y Margaret*. New York: Greenwillow Books, 1993. Margaret speaks only English, and Margarita speaks only Spanish. When they meet at the park, they become friends and teach one another how to speak their languages.

Rey, H. A. *Jorge el Curioso* (Curious George). Translated by Pedro Villa Fernandez. Boston: Houghton Mifflin, 1969. This Spanish edition of the children's classic features a complete Spanish-English vocabulary list at the back of the book and translations of new or difficult phrases at the foot of each page.

Say, Allen. *El Chino*. Boston: Houghton Mifflin, 1993. A biography of Bill Wong, a Chinese American who becomes a famous bullfighter in Spain.

———. *Grandfather's Journey*. Boston: Houghton Mifflin, 1993. In a beautifully illustrated tale, Allen Say tells the story of his grandfather's journey from Japan to America.

Seuss, Dr. *Oh, the Places You'll Go!* New York: Random House, 1990. Rhymed advice for proceeding in life; weathering fear, loneliness, and confusion; and being in charge of your actions.

———. *The Cat in the Hat Beginner Book Dictionary in Spanish*. Translated by Robert R. Nardelli. New York: Random House, 1966. Adaptation and translation of the picture dictionary, *The Cat in the Hat Dictionary*.

Smith, Robert Kimmel. *Chocolate Fever*. Illustrated by Gioia Fiammenghi. New York: Dell, 1978. After eating a large quantity of chocolate, Henry breaks out in brown bumps that help him thwart some hijackers and also teach him a lesson about self-indulgence.

Surat, Michele Maria. *Angel Child, Dragon Child*. Illustrated by Vo-Dinh Mai. New York: Scholastic, 1983. A Vietnamese girl attending school in the United States, lonely for her mother left behind in Vietnam, makes a new friend who helps her out in a surprising way.

Tafuri, Nancy. *Junglewalk*. New York: Greenwillow Books, 1988. After reading a book about jungle animals, a little boy falls asleep and meets the animals in his dream.

Tunis, Edwin. *Colonial Living*. New York: Thomas Y. Crowell, 1957. A visually rich text which depicts life in colonial times.

White, E. B. *Charlotte's Web*. Illustrated by Garth Williams. New York: Harper, 1952. Wilbur, the pig, is desolate when he learns that he is destined to be the farmer's Christmas dinner until his spider friend, Charlotte, decides to help him.

Wiesner, David. *Tuesday*. New York: Clarion Books, 1991. Frogs rise on their lily pads, float through the air, and explore the nearby houses while their inhabitants sleep.

Winter, Jeanette. *Follow the Drinking Gourd*. New York: Dragonfly, 1988. By following the directions in a song—"The Drinking Gourd"—runaway slaves journey north along the Underground Railroad to freedom in Canada.

Winter, Jeanette and Jonah. *Diego*. Illustrated by Jeanette Winter. New York: Knopf, 1991. This vibrantly illustrated bilingual book tells the story of one of Mexico's most famous artists—Diego Rivera—in a way that children can understand and enjoy. Each page of the book features a colorful miniature of one of Rivera's paintings.

Zhensun, Zheng and Alice Low. *A Young Painter*. Photographs by Zheng Zhensun. New York: Byron Press, 1991. This book examines the life and works of Wang Yani, the Chinese girl who became the youngest artist to have a one-person show at the Smithsonian Institution.

Professional Associations and Publications

The American Alliance for Health, Physical
Education, Recreation, and Dance (AAHPERD)
*Journal of Physical Education, Recreation,
and Dance*
1900 Association Drive
Reston, Virginia 22091

American Alliance for Theater and Education
(AATE)
AATE Newsletter
c/o Arizona State University Theater Department
Box 873411
Tempe, Arizona 85287

American Association for the Advancement
of Science (AAAS)
Science Magazine
1333 H Street NW
Washington, DC 20005

American Association of Colleges for Teacher
Education (AACTE)
AACTE Briefs
1 DuPont Circle NW, Suite 610
Washington, DC 20036

American Association of School Administrators
(AASA)
The School Administrator
1801 North Moore Street
Arlington, Virginia 22209

Association for Childhood Education
International (ACEI)
*Childhood Education: Infancy Through
Early Adolescence*
11141 Georgia Avenue, Suite 200
Wheaton, Maryland 20902

Association for Supervision and Curriculum
Development (ASCD)
Educational Leadership
1250 North Pitt Street
Alexandria, Virginia 22314

California Association for Bilingual Education (CABE)
660 South Figueroa Street, Suite 1040
Los Angeles, California 90017

The Council for Exceptional Children (CEC)
Teaching Exceptional Children
1920 Association Drive
Reston, Virginia 22091

Education Theater Association (ETA)
Dramatics
3368 Central Parkway
Cincinnati, Ohio 45225

International Reading Association (IRA)
The Reading Teacher
800 Barksdale Road
Newark, Delaware 19714

Music Educators National Conference (MENC)
Music Educators Journal
1806 Robert Fulton Drive
Reston, Virginia 22091

National Art Education Association (NAEA)
Art Education
1916 Association Drive
Reston, Virginia 22091

National Association for Bilingual Education (NABE)
1220 L Street NW, Suite 605
Washington, DC 20005

National Association for the Education
of Young Children (NAEYC)
Young Children
1509 16th Street NW
Washington, DC 20036

National Association of Elementary School
Principals (NAESP)
Communicator
1615 Duke Street
Alexandria, Virginia 22314

National Center for Restructuring Education,
Schools, and Teaching (NCREST)
Resources for Restructuring
P.O. Box 110
Teachers College, Columbia University
New York, New York 10027

National Council for the Social Studies (NCSS)
Social Education
Social Studies and the Young Learner
3501 Newark Street NW
Washington, DC 20016

National Council of Supervisors of Mathematics
(NCSM)
*NCSM Newsletter Leadership in Mathematics
Education*
P.O. Box 10667
Golden, Colorado 80401

National Council of Teachers of English (NCTE)
Language Arts
Primary Voices K-6
1111 Kenyon Road
Urbana, Illinois 61801

National Council of Teachers of Mathematics
(NCTM)
Arithmetic Teacher
Teaching Children Mathematics
1906 Association Drive
Reston, Virginia 22091

National Dance Association (NDA)
Spotlight on Dance
1900 Association Drive
Reston, Virginia 22091

National Science Teachers Association (NSTA)
Science and Children
Science for Children: Resources for Teachers
1840 Wilson Boulevard
Arlington, Virginia 22201

National Storytelling Association (NSA)
P.O. Box 309
Jonesborough, Tennessee 37659

Phi Delta Kappa
Phi Delta Kappan
408 North Union
Bloomington, Indiana 47402

Society for Research in Music Education
Journal for Research in Music Education
c/o Music Educators National Conference
1806 Robert Fulton Drive
Reston, Virginia 22091

The Southern Poverty Law Center
Teaching Tolerance
400 Washington Avenue
Montgomery, Alabama 36104

Teachers of English to Speakers of Other
Languages (TESOL)
TESOL Newsletter
1600 Cameron Street, Suite 300
Alexandria, Virginia 22314

The Strategies for Teaching and Learning Professional Library

Administrators Supporting School Change
Robert Wortman
1-57110-047-4   paperback

Bob Wortman is a talented elementary school principal who writes with conviction and humor of his goals and strategies as a principal in this book directed at all who are interested in school revitalization, especially administrators and curriculum supervisors.

Bob explains the importance of having a vision and philosophy as well as a practical understanding of how people learn, an ability to make use of time and organization, and a concern for maintaining positive relationships with all members of the school community-parents, students, and teachers.

Assessment: Continuous Learning
Lois Bridges
1-57110-048-2   paperback

Effective teaching begins with knowing your students, and assessment is a learning tool that enables you to know them. Indeed, the real power of continuous assessment is that it informs your teaching and helps you decide what to do next.

This book provides a wide range of teacher-developed kidwatching and assessment forms to show different ways to reflect on children's work. It offers developmental checklists, student and child interview suggestions, guidelines for using portfolios, rubrics, and self-evaluation profiles. Also included are *Dialogues* that invite reflection, *Shoptalks* that offer lively reviews of the best and latest professional literature, and *Teacher-To-Teacher Field Notes* offering tips from practicing educators.

Creating Your Classroom **Community**
Lois Bridges
1-57110-049-0   paperback

Chances are the teachers you remember are those who really knew and cared for you as an unique individual with special interests, needs, and experiences. Now, as a teacher with your own classroom and students to care for, you'll want to create a classroom environment that supports each student as an individual while drawing the class together as a thriving learning community.

Creating Your Classroom Community offers the basics of effective elementary school teaching:

- how to create a classroom that supports what we know about learning;
- how to help each of your students to develop and practice self-responsibility;
- how to organize your classroom workspace to best support learning;
- how to construct a curriculum that focuses on your teaching and evaluation methods;
- how to turn to parents and the larger community for classroom support.

Dance as a Way of Knowing

Jennifer Zakkai

1-57110-064-4   paperback

Jennifer Zakkai illuminates how and why dance is a powerful tool for creative learning in K–6 classrooms. Student will learn how to engage in structured learning experiences that demand a high level of concentration and creativity. You don't have to be a dancer to enjoy using the detailed model lessons that take your students through warm-ups, movement explorations, rich curricular integrations, culminating activities, observation, and reflection.

Drama as a Way of Knowing

Paul G. Heller

1-57110-050-4   paperback

You don't have to be a Broadway actor to use drama in your classroom. There's plenty of dramatic energy in your students already, and Paul Heller shows you how to turn it into an effective learning tool.

Through his Ten-Step Process in which you, the teacher, are the director, he shows what you should do to guide your students through rewarding dramatic experiences. You'll find out how to use drama techniques to enable students to access and explore the curriculum in ways that promote deeper thinking. Moving beyond techniques, he also presents the nuts and bolts of pantomime and improvisation, of writing and acting scenes, even creating and presenting large-scale productions.

Literature as a Way of Knowing

Kathy G. Short

1-57110-063-6   paperback

Basal programs cannot provide the variety and choice of reading materials that meet students' needs. Stories that are worth reading and that extend children's experiences and enrich their minds also motivate them to make reading part of their lives. Kathy Short outlines the four roles literature plays in the curriculum and shows you how to use real books to help children learn. She concludes with a discussion of evaluation as part of the curriculum and offers specific examples of evaluation techniques and samples of appropriate forms.

Math as a Way of Knowing
Susan Ohanian

1-57110-051-2   paperback

Award-winning author Susan Ohanian conducts a lively tour of classrooms around the country where "math time" means stimulating learning experiences. To demonstrate that mathematics is an active, ongoing way of perceiving and interacting with the world, she explores teaching mathematical concepts through hands-on activities, writing and talking about what numbers mean, and discovering the where and why of math in everyday life.

Focusing on the NCTM's Standards, Susan takes you into classrooms for a firsthand look at exciting ways the standards are implemented. For the nonspecialist in particular, Susan shows that math really is an exciting and powerful tool that students can readily understand and apply.

Music as a Way of Knowing
Nick Page

1-57110-052-0   paperback

Rich with ideas on how to use music in the classroom, *Music as a Way of Knowing* will appeal especially to classroom teachers who are not musicians, but who enjoy and learn from music and want to use it with their students. Indeed, Nick Page reveals the truth of the adage "If you can talk, you can sing. If you can walk, you can dance."

Nick provides simple instructions for writing songs, using music to support learning across the curriculum, teaching singing effectively, and finding good songs. He assures you that with time, all students can sing well. The good news is that once you've read this book, you'll have the confidence to trust yourself and your students to sing and learn well through the joy and power of music.

Second Language Learners
Stephen Cary

1-57110-065-2   paperback

Stephen Cary helps K–5 teachers and administrators bring second language learners at all levels of English language proficiency into the core curriculum. With plenty of charts, visuals, and student samples as text support, Stephen shows you that comprehensible, engaging instruction means SSL kids acquire more content and more language. Whether involved in SLL program planning, coordinating staff-development workshops, or teaching in an elementary classroom, you'll find an abundance of ideas in this book.

Writing as a Way of Knowing
Lois Bridges

1-57110-062-8   paperback

You can help your students become flexible writers who understand all that writing can do and who know how to use it to serve their own purposes.

With Lois Bridges as your guide, you'll explore the many ways to develop young writers:

- how to run a writer's workshop;
- how to implement effective mini-lessons;
- how to conduct thought-provoking writing conferences;
- how to handle revising, editing, and publishing;
- how to recognize the qualities of effective writing.

Lois also explains how to teach the basic skills within the context of real writing, and how to help young writers monitor their own use of conventional spelling, punctuation, and grammar. She covers writing as it applies throughout the curriculum in a chapter on students as independent researchers, tracking down, sorting, and presenting data in a wide variety of formats, and outlines a four-step instructional strategy for introducing new genres, including journal writing and poetry.